To Maureen
birthday. May this little
book be a reminder of
your many blessings.
With our love always,
Mom & Dad
8/28/09

Counting Blessings

Counting
Blessings

Kerry Blair

Covenant Communications

Cover image by Janis Christie © 2008 Getty Images
Cover design copyrighted 2008 by Covenant Communications, Inc.
Published by Covenant Communications, Inc.
American Fork, Utah

Printed in Canada
First Printing: March 2008

15 14 13 12 11 10 09 08   10 9 8 7 6 5 4 3 2 1

ISBN 10: 1-59811-558-8
ISBN 13: 978-1-59811-558-1

Preface and Dedication

I want to keep the commandments. I do a pretty good job with some of the biggies. *Thou shalt not kill.* No problem. *Tithing.* Check. It's some of the others that occasionally cause me to falter. And when it comes to keeping a journal, I fall flat on my face. I've started at least two dozen in my life and filled . . . hold on a minute, let me count . . . zero.

Rather ironic for a writer, don't you think?

But I do love to write letters. I think it's because there's less pressure. (Doesn't the whole "writing for generations yet to come" thing make *you* freeze up?) So, when a friend suggested that instead of a journal to posterity I write weekly letters to people currently sharing a turn on earth with me, I found the idea both intriguing and doable. Thus began a year-long experience in introspection—a journal of epistles that I call *Counting Blessings.*

Because letters must be written to someone (and because "Dear Diary" sounds so middle school), each of these letters was written to . . . well . . . *you*. Just as Jane Austen addressed a "Gentle Reader" in her novels, I wrote these letter-essays with you in mind. Correct me if I'm wrong, but I picture you as someone a lot like me—a woman who wears more hats than Queen Elizabeth. (But not always with her aplomb!) We are daughters, wives, mothers, sisters, aunts, friends, neighbors, homemakers, breadwinners, students, Primary workers, PTA presidents, camp directors, Sunday School teachers, soccer moms, community volunteers, leaders, followers, strugglers, believers—heavenly queens-in-embryo. We are legion . . . and we are exhausted.

Martha in action, we are Mary at heart.

While writing to you was an exercise in personal enlightenment and a joy besides, compiling my personal correspondence for the perusal of anybody with ten bucks or a library card turned out to be simply terrifying. I mean, honestly, would *you* be willing to set *your* journal out on bookshelves around the world?

My hope is that this will turn out to be a lot like writing fiction—but with fewer plot twists. The truth is, when I first began a "career" as a novelist, I had no idea how to go about that either. I'd never taken a creative writing class or read an LDS novel. Writing a book that was accepted and published was like tumbling down a rabbit hole after Alice. Sending out this book of letters to you feels the same way. It's as if I'm standing at the top of a bottomless black hole, looking down in apprehension. Do I really want to go there? If I do, how do I get in? How well I empathize with the protagonist in George MacDonald's *Dealings with the Fairies.*[1]

> *The Old Man of the Earth stooped over the floor of the cave, raised a huge stone from it, and left it leaning. It disclosed a great hole that went plumb-down.*
>
> *"That is the way," he said.*
>
> *"But there are no stairs."*
>
> *"You must throw yourself in. There is no other way."*

Isn't that true of most worthwhile endeavors, artistic and otherwise? In order to succeed at almost anything, we must close our eyes, screw our courage to the sticking place, and throw ourselves in. There is seldom any other way.

---

[1] MacDonald, George, "The Golden Key," *Dealings with the Fairies* (London: Alexander Strahan & Co., 1868).

But why do it? Why venture into that dark hole of uncertainty and possible failure in the first place? Kate Douglas Wiggin answered that question in *Rebecca of Sunnybrook Farm*:

> *Going to Aunt Mirandy's is like going down cellar in the dark. There might be ogres and giants under the stairs,—but, as I tell Hannah, there might be elves and fairies and enchanted frogs!*[2]

I began writing to see if I could find the elves and fairies and enchanted frogs that I hoped might exist somewhere down that deep, dark rabbit hole of ambition. While I've come across a metaphorical ogre now and again—and am still fighting a giant inferiority complex—I've been blessed with happy endings just the same. The magic, of course, has come in the form of the loyal allies, golden Geese, and fairy godpersons I've encountered along the way. Long have I been blessed by my association with the good folk at Covenant Communications. (If you never find a magic lamp, let me assure you that stumbling upon a truly marvelous publisher is the next best thing!) Most recently I encountered Kathryn Gille, a young woman with a remarkable gift. Kat can spin dry-as-straw

---

[2] Wiggin, Kate Douglas, "We Are Seven," *Rebecca of Sunnybrook Farm* (New York: Grosset & Dunlap, 1903), 8.

essays into something that, if not gold, are infinitely shinier than they were when she first picked them up. With wonderful editors being as rare as genies these days, I'm so grateful she inherited me when the remarkable Angela Eschler moved on to dream-fulfill elsewhere.

This book, then, is dedicated to the aforementioned, and to Sariah, who presented the idea; Stephanie, who pulled me to the brink; Jennie and Jeff, who gave me a gentle shove every time I tried to edge away from the black hole; Cheri and La Merle, who keep me going no matter what fears may come; and, Gentle Reader, it is dedicated to you—most of all to you—with appreciation, admiration, and love for the way you shoulder the yoke, lead the way, and bring joy to the journey.

Part 1:
Counting Blessings

So, amid the conflict whether great or small,

Do not be disheartened, God is over all;

Count your many blessings, angels will attend,

Help and comfort give you to your journey's end.

—Johnson Oatman Jr., "Count Your Many Blessings,"
Songs for Young People, 1897

It's About Time

Next year I will be thirty-five years old—since I took weekends off.

I stole that line from a movie I saw this week. The character it was said to did the math in his head in less than five seconds. I couldn't do it in five days if you gave me a calendar and a graphing calculator. (And I'm counting on the fact that you couldn't either, or I wouldn't have brought it up.) But the mathematical equation isn't the point. The point is that considering how looooooong I've been around, shouldn't I have learned to use my time wisely by now?

As Latter-day Saints we are practically obsessed with anxiously engaging ourselves in good causes. Maybe it's subliminal. Glancing through the hymnal last Sunday, I noted that as sisters in Zion, we who are called to serve are all enlisted to go marching, marching forward because the world has need of willing men to all press on scattering sunshine. We wonder if we have done any good in the world today, because we have been given much and want to do what is right, keep the commandments, press forward with the Saints, and put our shoulders to the wheel going where He wants us to go. However, as the morning breaks high on the mountain top, truth reflects upon our senses, and while we still believe that sweet is the work, we also realize that we have work enough to do ere the sun goes down. And thus we ask Thee ere we part, where can we turn for peace?

Peace for me would be the reassurance that I am indeed choosing the right. For instance, in the time it will take me to write this letter, I could write a couple of pages of a new novel, read twenty pages of scripture, iron six of my husband's shirts, run a hundred ancestral names through TempleReady, weed my garden, compose a sonnet, write my congressman, prepare my Primary lesson, exercise, drive one-third of the way to the Mesa Temple, babysit for an ill neighbor, respond at last to that pesky computerized voice that keeps saying "you've got mail," bake bread, visit teach 2.36 of the sisters on my list, bathe the dog/brush the cat/clean the fish tank, or cure cancer.

Okay, that last one is about as likely as ironing my husband's shirts. (I just threw those two in to see if you were paying attention.) But the rest of the list is plausible—and it goes on and on. The thing is, I'd like to do all of those things (okay, most of them) and more. Unfortunately, I've developed an annoying habit of sleeping seven or eight hours a day. No matter what I do in the remaining sixteen or seventeen hours, I still tend to feel guilty about what I *don't* do.

And sometimes I feel guilty about what I *do* do—even when I'm actively trying to choose the right. Remember that movie I mentioned watching? I should also have told you that while I watched it I copied the Ten Commandments onto eight 1 x 2-foot slabs of sandstone.

That's eighty commandments. I think I've got them down now.

The guilt comes in wondering, *Now that I've done all that commandment copying, do I have a stack of memorable handouts for my Primary class or a small sandstone monument to a colossal waste of two hours?*

In another thirty-five years—still taking weekends and major holidays off—maybe I'll have this time-management thing figured out. If not, maybe I'll at least be able to write a pamphlet titled "Ten Terrific Tips to Rid Your Life of Guilt." If ever I do accomplish either of those things, I'll get back to you. In the meantime, I guess I'll continue to do what I suspect you do: keep my hands to work and my heart to God.

At least I'll try. That little plaque hanging in my kitchen makes it sound a whole lot easier than it is.

My Mother's Days Are All Wet

If I have a claim to fame, it might be that I was baptized on Mother's Day. Twice. Both baptisms were more or less against my will, although the second dunking was for a good cause—to prevent a death in the family.

To appreciate this story, you must first know that I grew up surrounded by my grandmother's sisters: Olivia Yozelle (Zella), Thelma Iona (Toots), Wyona Elsie (Nona), and Pauline Esther (Polly). My grandmother's name was Dallace Alma, but everybody called her Dutchey. Maybe it was law in 1900-era Kansas that women couldn't be called by their given names. Or possibly, given these women's names, they all begged to be called something else. At any rate, the grande dame of the clan was their aunt, my Great-Great Aunt Dora (Dode), who was already ancient when I was born.

Aunt Dode was the only force on earth that could get my parents to church in their busy middle years—once a year, that is. Every Mother's Day, one or the other of them drove me and Aunt Dode to a tiny little church in a tiny little town about forty miles from where we lived. I'm not sure this is gospel truth, but I think Aunt Dode started going when she heard that each year the pastor presented a lovely wrapped gift to the oldest mother in the congregation. At any rate, one year Aunt Polly was visiting and went with us. It was she who saw to it that I was finally (and thoroughly) "saved"—despite my howled protests that I was really quite a happy little heathen. Thus befell my first Mother's Day baptism.

The year I turned sixteen, my parents decided that Aunt Dode and I were a match made in heaven. I could drive her to church, and they could devote one more Sunday each year to yard work. (The yard did not improve noticeably, I'm sorry to say.) Who could have foreseen that this would be the year my aunt would finally crave salvation along with that lovely wrapped gift?

It began innocently enough. After we were "comfortably" seated on the rough-hewn wooden benches, a chorister led us in a hymn. A deacon (not the twelve-year-old kind) led us in prayer. The pastor gave the sermon. More deacons (still of the geriatric persuasion) passed the collection plate. At last the service was over and it was time for all the mothers in the congregation to rise. Then, under the pastor's benevolent direction, everyone under the age of thirty sat down, followed by everybody under forty, and fifty, and so on. At last the only mother standing was Aunt Dode—and that was only because I was holding her up.

With her fame maintained yet another year—and her gift firmly in hand—I figured we were good to go. Except that the meeting wasn't over. It had merely been adjourned long enough to allow the congregation to make a fifty-yard trek to the riverbank, where we were to reassemble for a baptism. I was surprised. Possibly I was appalled. In the Methodist church that I regularly attended, less than an inch of water, sprinkled lightly, sufficed believers.

Not so with these people. Remembering vividly what had happened the last time I was present when these people sang "Shall We Gather at the River," I headed quickly for the car.

Unfortunately, Aunt Dode insisted on following the crowd. She loved to see people "dunked," she said, and she wasn't missing the show.

Ever the dutiful great-grandniece, I pushed her wheelchair across the meadow to the muddy banks of the Hassayampa River. There we gathered in tree-dappled sunlight, sang a hymn, recited the Lord's prayer, and listened to the pastor relate a truly touching account of our Savior's baptism in the River Jordan. It was one of the most moving experiences of my life. So moved was I that I didn't notice that my aunt had also moved—down the bank and into the pastor's arms to petition for baptism. As he looked at me over her thinning, snowy-white hair, I quickly did the calculations:

> *Cool, 70° weather*
> *Icy cold, muddy water*
> *+ Frail, 90-year-old woman*
> *―――――――――――――――*
> *2x pneumonia and certain death*

I could explain my lack of interference to my grandmother and formidable cadre of aunts at Dode's funeral.

Not.

I scrambled down the bank to retrieve her. Unfortunately, Lot's wife, post-pillar, would have been easier to reason with. Fortunately (or not) the pastor possessed the wisdom of Solomon. Surely, he told my aunt with evangelical zeal, the Lord had led her to the banks of salvation, but wasn't it possible that she was an instrument in His hands? Perhaps, after living a good life and finding favor in His sight, God's gift to her this Mother's Day was to be able to look on as her dear niece accepted His Son.

Me?

Here?

Again?

Come to think of it, it was probably only *sixty* degrees under all those cottonwoods, the creek undoubtedly contained more mud and leeches than water, and I didn't have dry clothes—or even a crumpled Kleenex to dry off with. Nevertheless, as you already know because I gave away the punch line in the second paragraph, I drove home soggy, muddy . . . and probably happier than I'd ever been.

Believe it or not, I did the "dunking" thing again three springs later, and yet again, five springs after that. (It was different those last two times, though— eternally different, thanks to priesthood authority.) Stepping into the warm, crystal clear waters of a font in the Mesa Temple, I was baptized for my grandmother, Aunt Nona, Aunt Zella, Aunt Toots, and, of course, Aunt Dode. The temple experience was glorious—and leech free!—and I knew absolutely that my marvelous great-great aunt was happy and anxious and very near, grateful to accept the most valuable Mother's Day gift she'd ever been given.

How grateful *I* was to be there with her yet again. After all, as claims to fame go, mine is probably the best one to have.

Can We Talk?

Call me an addict, but I watched five hours of television this week (May 2007). Four hours were about the Mormons, and one hour was about people in Herculaneum in AD 79. Both programs were produced by PBS. I liked the second one better, but nobody in America is talking about Herculaneumians. Everybody's talking about Mormons instead.

As of this morning, PBS had logged more than two thousand responses to Helen Whitney's documentary "The Mormons." *The Washington Post* received almost double that number after carrying a live chat with the producer. The Church's website says its hits have increased tenfold. Church leaders have not only responded quickly, publicly, and mostly positively—albeit carefully—to the show's airing, but they've also opened a forum for discussion.

Apparently I'm the only one who doesn't want to talk about "The Mormons." With apologies to PBS, *The Washington Post,* and the LDS public affairs office, after thirty years as the only Mormon in my extended family, well, I'm just all talked out.

One month from today marks the anniversary of my baptism. I was nineteen, and a feminist history major with a pre-law 4.0 average. (In other words, I thought I was an intellectual.) I was also close kin to someone who stood on street corners declaring to all who would listen that Mormons are the spawn of Satan.

(*Stood* is past-tense in that last sentence only because my Great-Aunt Polly has passed away. If she were still alive, she'd still be standing on street corners, handing out anti-Mormon tracts. For years, when a bishop or stake president asked if I had any association with people actively trying to destroy the Church, I'd respond sheepishly, "Does Thanksgiving count?")

Surrounded by loved ones like Aunt Polly, a new Mormon can do a lot of talking. (Especially when one is talking to the biological equivalent of a fence post.) About twenty years into my conversion, I grew tired of telling my family why I was still a Latter-day Saint and decided to write about it instead. My first book, *The Heart Has Its Reasons,* is a conversion story—in some ways my conversion story—disguised as romantic fiction. It's not, therefore, erroneous to conclude that I would not be an author if only I were a better missionary.

If I learned anything from television this week (besides some rather frightening facts about Mount Vesuvius), it's that one witness of the Spirit is worth a thousand words from scholars, naysayers, and cultural historians. In "The Mormons," polygamy, priesthood, and Mountain Meadows were sensationalized (as usual), but Elder Jensen and the smattering of members interviewed were simply sensational. (Those people glowed brighter than Moroni in an old Church video.) I looked at the members who represented us to America and saw intelligent, humble, happy people who had put Christ at the center of their lives—people with enough faith, hope, and love to build boats and move mountains if the need ever again arose.

I'm firmly convinced that the thousands of positive responses to the documentary are due largely to nonmembers responding to our members. Who would you want to worship with or live next door to? The intellectual? The scholar? The person who wouldn't recognize truth and compassion if she tripped over it in an empty room? I'll take the drug addict who let Christ heal her soul; the widower father who doesn't understand the Lord's will but accepts it anyway; and the talented young woman who faces early death with a smile on her face and her eyes firmly fixed on eternal life. If these are Latter-day Saints—and they are!—thank heaven I associated myself with them when I did.

And I *do* thank heaven that I found the gospel. I thank God every single day of my life. (Well, okay . . . there *was* this string of early mornings at girls' camp once when I fervently wished I were still a Methodist!) My conversion was fast, admittedly, but it wasn't easy. There is probably nobody in the kingdom today who had a harder time than I did believing that story about the farm kid in upstate New York. And yet I did believe it. Do believe it. In Primary we're learning an incredibly beautiful song, "This is My Beloved Son," about the Father bearing witness of the divinity of Jesus Christ. The third verse begins:

> *Joseph saw two glorious beings,*
> *Shining brighter than the sun.*
> *God again presented Jesus:*
> *"This is My Beloved Son . . ."[3]*

I'm so sure this statement is true that each time I try to sing it, my throat constricts. Still, it is the final verse that truly resonates within me:

---

[3] Gardner, Marvin K., "This Is My Beloved Son," *Children's Songbook* (Salt Lake City: The Church of Jesus Christ of Latter-day Saints, 1989), 76.

As I read the scriptures daily,
Words of Christ, the Holy One,
In my heart I'll hear God tell me:
"This is my Beloved Son."

I can't explain it better than that—although I've been trying for three decades now. I read the Book of Mormon, I listened to the missionaries, and in my heart I heard God tell me, *This is the Church of My Beloved Son.* All the documentaries—and commentaries on the documentaries, and commentaries on the commentaries on the documentaries—can't possibly impact that witness.

I'm still writing books, as you can see, but now I'm doing it in the hopes of putting a little money aside in case I get a chance to be a full-time missionary someday. And if I don't, well, there's always Aunt Polly to work on. I'm sure she's waiting for me on the other side of the veil. I'm not worried anymore. I'm not only better prepared to talk to her now, but I've done enough temple work for our shared ancestors that I think I can count on a few reinforcements!

And isn't loving our family, our Father's family— all of them, at all times and in all times—what being a Mormon is all about?

I just wish I knew how to go about doing the temple work for all those people in Herculaneum. After all, they're the ones I'm really worried about.

The Sands of Time

What have you been doing for the last quarter century?

You wouldn't believe how often I'm asked that. I think it's because I didn't publish my first novel until I was forty. People want to know what I did all those years I didn't write. The truth is, I *did* write. Besides eight novels, I've written two roadshows, four stake productions, a few dozen PE excuses, almost a hundred Teacher Appreciation Day notes, more than my share of Cub Scout and girls' camp skits, and about a dozen journal entries in the form of letters to the cosmos—counting this one. I have ghostwritten for Santa Claus, the Tooth Fairy, and the ghost of a gerbil that I claimed "ran away for an exciting new life in the city." (There was a cat in our home that knew otherwise.) I have also collaborated on dozens of Primary talks and more late-night school reports than I really *should* have.

Of course, my adult life has not been all literary achievement. After all, I've shared a home with one husband, four children, two parents, eight dogs, five cats, nine rabbits, one cockatiel, four parakeets, a box turtle, a swimming turtle, six hermit crabs, five hamsters, nine gerbils (they're prolific little critters), four ducks, fifteen chickens, and pet fish, frogs, finches, and bugs too numerous to mention. (I fear that if it is true that we receive our "beloved" pets back in the eternities, the only family we will be fit to live next door to will be Noah's.) But my point—and I do have one—is that along with all these people and animals I have loved have come certain domestic necessities. I have compiled a partial list:

When I wasn't writing I was changing diapers (about 14,600) and litter boxes (2,400) or washing 21,000 loads of laundry, preparing 27,325 meals (if one is generous enough to consider pouring milk on Cheerios and/or driving through McDonald's preparing a meal), and cleaning toilets about 950 times. (Don't do the math on that last one, or you will never enter a bathroom in my home!)

In my spare time I've logged enough carpool mileage to have driven to Mars and back. I've rooted for the underdogs at pint-sized sporting events that lasted longer than the summer Olympics, and I've sat enthralled through three-hour concerts in which one of my kids played the triangle—off-key and at the wrong tempo. I've served on ten PTA boards at six different schools, chaired enough carnivals to make P.T. Barnum blanch, outsold Amazon.com at school bookfairs, and discussed with kindergarteners the entire holdings of the Metropolitan Museum of Art in the Mesa Public School Art Masterpiece program. Of course, it hasn't been all work and no play. I wore out two copies of *The Cat in the Hat* when my kids were preschoolers, and I later read all seven volumes of *The Chronicles of Narnia.* Aloud. Twice. I've orchestrated quality time with my family at Disneyland, Sea World, the Grand Canyon, Mesa General Hospital's emergency room, and the US Marine Corps's boot camp graduation.

In case you haven't guessed by now, I'm a mother. Not only that, I'm a veteran mother. I've survived the terrible twos and the fearsome fourteens, and I'm now facing the terrifying twenties. Over the years I've sent my kids off to preschool, Scout camp, first dates, the senior prom . . . and war in Iraq.

In short (although I know it's too late for that), I have spent the last twenty-five years of my life trying—and mostly failing—to be the kind of mother they extol in sacrament meetings. No fame. No fortune. Heck, I haven't even gotten enough sleep. But I can live with that. (Or, rather, without all that.) One of my favorite writers, the Apostle Neal A. Maxwell, wrote, "When the surf of centuries has made the great pyramids so much sand, the everlasting family will still be standing, because it is a celestial institution, formed outside telestial time."[4]

Thank goodness. There's never been enough telestial time to accomplish everything I think I should do. (Like write. Or sleep.) Thank you, Elder Maxwell, for the assurance to all of us mothers that every late night, every early morning—every single minute—of mothering is the best way we could possibly spend our lives.

So that's what I've been doing for the last quarter century, and I'd do it all over again in a heartbeat. Well, almost all of it. If I really had do-overs, I'd make sure that *both* gerbils were females before I left the pet shop.

This essay was previously published in a slightly different form as "The Noblest Vocation" in Of Infinite Worth *(American Fork, Utah: Covenant Communications, Inc, 2007).*

---

[4] Maxwell, Neal A., "The Women of God," *Ensign*, May 1978, 10.

Five Words I Met on the Way to Heaven

In the parable of the talents, a wealthy man gathers three of his servants and entrusts them with his goods while he is away. To one he gives five talents, to another two, and to a third he gives one talent—each according to their abilities. As you probably recall, the first two servants doubled what they were given while the third servant dug a pit in the earth and hid his talent in order to "keep it safe."

Do you ever wonder if Luke missed somebody when he retold the tale? In latter-day revelation, and indeed, in His life's teachings, Christ makes it clear there is a *fourth* type of servant. While some workers dig pits and others go merrily on their way multiplying their talents little or much, there are yet others who pause in the enrichment of the fortune the Master has entrusted to them to consider the plight of those around them. When they see a fellow servant hide up his talent, they drop what they are doing and rush to help.

I know this kind of person well. The Master has often set them along my path because He knows that I am, without doubt, a well-meaning but easily discouraged and sometimes foolish handmaid. Having raised "careful and troubled about many things" to an art form, I too often stand frozen, my talent clutched in a sweaty palm, because I'm frankly unsure just *what* to do with it. (When Luke called this kind of mortal mania "cumbered," he certainly knew whereof he spoke. And I'm not just saying that to make up for pointing out his possible journalistic oversight earlier.)

Frankly, I'd hoped since childhood to use any meager talent I might have been given to eke out a career as a writer. Even though writing was a passion, I was so careful and troubled about things like school and marriage and children and callings and . . . *whatever* . . . that any talent I might have had ended up under a rock. (More accurately, it was buried under a veritable avalanche of the minutiae of life.) That little talent would still be buried today if it weren't for one of my best friends, Joan, who is truly one of those fourth types of servants.

Not only did Joan first encourage me to write, she dragged me along to her writer's group and applauded my first pathetic attempts at novelizationing. (I suspect that's not a word.) In metaphorical words, she stooped to dig my one tarnished talent out of the dirt, and she did it each and every time I dropped it. (Stepped on it. Buried it. Abandoned it forever.) Joan knew me well. She recognized that I was determined, if not destined, to spend my life obsessing about my lack of talent, or endlessly comparing myself with people who obviously had more talents than I, rather than using the measly gift I did have to help build the kingdom of God.

One day, in total frustration, she yelled at me, "Just write a stupid book!"

Turns out those are five of the most meaningful words I've heard on my journey toward the Light. They were so wise, in fact, that I wrote them down and still have them framed and sitting on my desk. *Don't obsess,* they remind me. *Don't despair. If you must be careful, be careful not to borrow trouble. Just write a stupid book now and worry about being a no-talent loser later.*

That simple phrase has so much power—it's worked nine times for me—that I've thought of copyrighting it and selling posters of the motto at writers' conferences worldwide. (But I'll give it to you free of charge today, just for reading my letters. You're welcome.)

There are so many servants like Joan—incredibly talented people who go about their Master's business in the way He intended. While magnifying their own talents all out of proportion, these people still take every opportunity to teach and bless, to build and edify others. If I started to name everybody who has profoundly affected me, I'd need an extra hundred pages—at least. So instead I'll silently bless their names (as I do every day) and wait to sing their praises until I get to the other side of the veil. (And take voice lessons.)

In the meantime, I'll try to dig my talent out from under that rock where I keep stashing it, polish it up a little, and use it whenever and wherever I can to follow the example of those fourth types of servants I so admire. They, more than the supposedly super-talented overachievers of this world, are the ones I know will hear: "Well done, thou good and faithful servant: thou hast been faithful over a few things, I will make thee ruler over many things: enter thou into the joy of thy lord" (Matthew 25:23).

A Bequest of Wings

Bad things do happen to good people. Sometimes the worst things happen to the best people. Right now, a handful of the best people I know are facing the most difficult things I can imagine—cancer, the serious illness of a parent, abandonment and divorce, and the death of a child. I wish I knew what to say to them.

My life is easy in comparison, but there have been some low points. One of the lowest was the day I was diagnosed with multiple sclerosis. I couldn't understand why God let this awful thing happen to me. Hadn't I tried hard enough? Been "good" enough? I couldn't talk to anyone here on earth about my pain and fear and lack of faith, and I was barely on speaking terms with God. About all I could manage in my prayers was, "What now? How do I get through this?"

God answered me in the words of my favorite poet, Emily Dickinson, who wrote:

Read, sweet, how others strove,
Till we are stouter;
What they renounced,
Till we are less afraid.[5]

That quatrain became my lifeline. As Emily suggested, I read the words of "brave men" and "celestial women" who "bore the faithful witness" through the ages. As I did, I gained perspective and strength.

One woman I encountered while following Emily's advice was Dame Julian of Norwich. In 1342 she wrote, "God allows some of us to fall more heavily and more grievously. And then we, who are not all-wise, think that everything which we have undertaken was all for nothing. But it is not so, for if we did not fall we could not know so completely the wonderful love of our Creator. We shall truly see that we were never hurt in His love, nor were we ever of less value in His sight."[6]

I figured if that was true in the dark ages of the fourteenth century, it was probably still true in the

[5] Dickinson, Emily, "XVIII," *Emily Dickinson Collected Poems* (Philadelphia: Running Press, 1991), 27.

[6] Dame Julian of Norwich, "The Revelation of Divine Love," *Julian of Norwich: Showings (Classics of Western Spirituality)*, comp. Edmund Colledge, James Walsh, and Jean Leclercq (New Jersey: Paulist Press, 1977).

twentieth. I began to look for things I could do instead of mourning everything I couldn't. I could still sit, for instance—for very long periods of time, in fact—and I had always wanted to write a book. About eighteen months after my diagnosis, my first novel was published.

I still search for words of inspiration when I'm afraid. (And frankly, because of CNN, that's pretty much every day.) I keep a quote from Margery Wilson in my journal. In 1917, the world contemplated the War to End All Wars. Margery wrote:

> *Though life seems to challenge us harshly at times, to make us eat bitter bread with the sweet, nevertheless, if we will stop wailing and look we will see a sustaining arm across our shoulders, the arm of infinite love—and if we listen we can hear a voice whispering, "Deep within you is the strength to bear anything, the nobility to be willing to do so, and the intelligence to create magnificently and beautifully, come what may."*[7]

Possibly I should admit that not every piece of writerly advice I cherish is touching and profound. I often quote these words by children's author Walter

---

[7] Wilson, Margery, "First Essentials," *The Woman You Want to Be* (Philadelphia and New York: J.B. Lippincott Company, 1942), 27; originally published in 1928 by The Margery Wilson Institute.

Brooks: "When life's at its darkest and everything's black, I don't want my friends to come patting my back. I scorn consolation, can't they let me alone? I just want to snivel, sob, bellow, and groan."[8]

Whether I've chosen to snivel through or survive my own challenges, the written words of others have seen me through the darkest and scariest days of my life. When I'm most stressed, I reach for an old friend on the bookshelf, and things seem better right away.

Well, most of the time. A couple of years ago, I took my husband to the hospital after he had a mild heart attack. Knowing he'd be in tests most of the day, and fearing to be left alone to worry, I snatched up a well-worn paperback to help keep me sane. As I sat in Gary's cubicle in the emergency room, I struggled to keep my eyes on the pages, because I was terrified of all the tubes and machines that were connected to the man I love. Nurses and doctors came and went, and each gave me a curious look. Hadn't they ever seen anybody read before?

Finally, my long-suffering husband sat up and said, "Do you have to read that right now?" Startled, I closed the book. Looking down at the cover, I saw that it was a copy of William Faulkner's *As I Lay Dying*.

Oops.

---

[8] Brooks, Walter R., *Freddy Goes to Florida* (New York: Overlook Press, 1997), 26.

The point is that William, Emily, Dame Julian, Margery, et al, have helped me through the darkest, scariest days of my life. Another of Emily's poems describes me to a T:

[She] ate and drank the precious words,
[Her] spirit grew robust;
[She] knew no more that [she] was poor,
Nor that [her] frame was dust.
[She] danced along the dingy days,
And this bequest of wings
Was but a book. What liberty
A loosened spirit brings![9]

[9] Dickinson, Emily, "XXI," *Emily Dickinson Collected Poems* (Philadelphia: Running Press, 1991), 28.

Do Drop in for a Spell

One cloudy October afternoon of the year I turned twelve, I ventured across the street from my house, pushed my way through the reedy honey-suckle vines that had been left to run wild, and climbed thirteen stairs to the witch's front door. There I rapped lightly and waited to be turned into a toad for my audacity. Everyone I knew, young and old alike, shunned the old woman who lived in that house. I always had too, but that particular day I was a girl on a mission. I was selling magazines. If I sold just two more, I would qualify for the grand-prize drawing for a portable TV. Unfortunately, every house in our small town had already been canvassed by prize-crazed adolescents.

Every house except the witch's. Nobody went there.

I remember the day as if it were yesterday. Before I could sneeze, a miniature tiger wrapped itself around my ankles, purring so loud it sounded like a growl. The autumn breeze was cool on my bare arms, and I shivered. Or maybe it wasn't the wind that raised the goose bumps. Maybe it was fear.

The witch opened the door, and I stared in open-mouthed wonder. I'd never before seen white carpeting or black lacquer furniture; this was the olive-green/harvest-gold seventies, after all. And nobody I knew had red Oriental silks or a crystal chandelier, so a living room of gingerbread and gumdrops would have surprised me less. Even the sounds in the air were bewitching—Verdi, I learned later. The witch was appropriately garbed in a long, black sheath and wore slippers of emerald satin— presumably because the ruby ones belonged to her sister in the East.

I couldn't speak, but the old woman saw the brochure in my hand and took it from me. She invited me in and I went. It's not so surprising when you think about it. Gretel fell for the gingerbread. Snow White fell for the poisoned apple. I fell for the witch.

And I fell hard. It was four years before I left that enchanted parlor again anytime I didn't have to. I only left in the end because she left me first. Even the best witches are not immortal.

Ardena Leer (the most beautifully named enchantress since Morgan LeFay) introduced me to a world I never knew existed. I'd long been a reader, but I'd never dreamed there were books like hers. Leather bound, gilt-edged works of Emerson and Browning and Dickens, they were the source of her magic. All the beauty and all the wisdom in the world was at her fingertips. She wielded it with power, reverence, and great generosity.

In the first of many books she gave me—a small tome of Shakespearean sonnets—Ardena wrote in a spidery script: *Forsan et haec olim meminisse juvabit.* It was a spell of the strongest variety. She wouldn't tell me what it meant, and she extracted from me a promise that I would ask no one; I must learn to read the magic words for myself. Twelve university hours of Latin later, I am probably the only girl on my block who speaks a dead language. (Frankly, Latin hasn't done me much good in life, but I figure it might still come in handy when I die. I'll be able to take the gospel to any Romans Paul might have missed.)

I didn't realize it until I sat down to write this paragraph, but I've long subscribed to only two magazines besides the *Ensign*: *Writer's Digest* and *Smithsonian.* I probably don't have to tell you they're the same two the witch bought from me.

Alas, my carpet is regrettably beige and my furniture is shabby chic, but my slippers are emerald and my silk scarf is Oriental. I have copies of most of the books that were in Ardena's library, and Verdi is among my CDs. In my lap is a cat, purring so loud that it almost sounds like he's growling. The honeysuckle vines along my fence are dying back now, but I'll let them grow wild again next spring.

Every October—and many months besides—I think of Ardena Leer, town witch. While I'm not a crone quite yet, I'm getting there. At least I hope I am.

I'll Forgive, President Faust,
But I'll Never Forget

President James E. Faust, Second Counselor in the First Presidency, passed away on Friday, August 10, 2007. These thoughts were recorded that morning.

Like many younger Saints, I've never seen a general conference where President Faust wasn't seated somewhere on the stand. (Yes, I was born before his call as a General Authority, but I wasn't reborn in the waters of baptism until almost a decade after it.) In other words, I've been moved by his testimony and touched by his spirit as long as I can remember. President Faust's passing feels like the loss of a surrogate grandfather, a wise and beloved friend, as well as a prophet of God. I am saddened today for me—for all of us—but thrilled to ponder the welcome he has received in the arms of our Savior.

I remember the first time I saw President Faust—or, indeed, any General Authority. I was a convert of about a dozen weeks, newly enrolled at BYU. The first Saturday in October rolled around, and one of my roommates happily shared the news that we could sleep in the next day because of general conference.

I'd never heard of it. (Don't blame yourselves, Elders Adams and Montgomery. Thanks to you, I went from clueless about the Church to a member-in-good-standing in six days. With a crash course like that, an infobit or two was bound to slip through the cracks in my gospel education.) At any rate, my roommate briefly explained the general idea of general conference.

I was stunned.

Awestruck.

Lot's wife, post-pillar.

When I could speak again, I said, "You mean *prophets* and *apostles* actually stand up to speak *tomorrow*, and *anybody* can be in the *same* room with *them* and listen and *see* them and *everything?*"

(My speech overflowed with italics in my youth. I'm better now. Not.)

My roommate yawned. "Anybody who gets there early enough, I guess."

I couldn't believe it. In junior high we'd written essays on "The Historical Figure I'd Most Like to

Meet." I'd chosen Peter—and been laughed out of homeroom. Now someone was telling me I could sit at the feet of a latter-day prophet and fourteen more Apostles besides?

Me? In the same place?

At the same time?

With *them*?

I went post-pillar again.

When I regained my senses, I dressed hurriedly, ran out to my car, and drove to Salt Lake City—all the while praying I would make it in time to claim one of the last places in line. I was even willing to sit on a window ledge like that boy in Acts who listened to Paul preach. (Unlike that kid, though, I wouldn't fall asleep and fall out the window, thus necessitating a break in proceedings while President Hinckley raised me from the dead.)

I arrived at the front gate of Temple Square at 12:07 AM. The temple spires, glowing golden in the lightly falling snow, were the most beautiful sight I had ever seen. I was awestruck by the pervading sense of peace. All was calm. All was bright. I looked around. A little too calm, come to think of it. I pushed against the high, wrought-iron gate. Locked. I dropped to the frozen ground in discouragement, certain I was the eleventh virgin. (You know, the one who had oil in her lamp but no alarm clock to get her to the wedding feast on time.)

It was nearing 1 AM when a security guard approached, pointed out that even homeless people were smart enough to be elsewhere, and suggested I move on.

I was incredulous. Obviously the man was an employee of the Church, but he hadn't heard about general conference! (Remarkably secretive, those Mormons.) I explained breathlessly that in a mere nine hours, prophets and apostles would assemble to speak to unworthy mortals like him and me, and all we had to do to get a seat was arrive early enough. Then I sadly explained that we were already too late. The place was deserted. The tabernacle must already be full.

He rolled his eyes heavenward and said, "You're a convert, aren't you?"

To this day I don't know how he knew, but I'm grateful he let me sit in an alcove outside the tabernacle, where it was a little warmer and a lot dryer. Turns out I was the first one in the building that morning.

(I know! I was surprised too!)

James E. Faust, a member of the Presidency of the Seventy, spoke that day on marriage. (No, my memory isn't that good. I looked it up on the Church website.) He said, "There is no great or majestic music which constantly produces the harmony of a great love. The most perfect music is a welding of two voices into one spiritual solo."[10] What a gift that man had for words. Truly a gift of the Spirit.

I don't show up for conference quite so early these days, but I always show up, if only in front of the TV. That's how I know that in his last conference, President Faust spoke on forgiveness. I won't relate his words here, because I know they're as deeply etched on your heart as they are on mine. I'll just say that since that talk I have been quicker to forgive, more anxious to understand, and more able to let go and move on and obtain peace. It was the last—and perhaps the greatest—gift given us by this remarkable, warm, tender, loving prophet of God.

When the tears finally dry, I know I will be able to forgive President Faust for leaving us so soon, but I will never, ever forget him.

---

[10] Faust, James E., "The Enriching of Marriage," *Ensign*, Nov 1977, 9–11; later reprinted as "Enriching Your Marriage," *Ensign*, April 2007, 4–6.

Part II: Counting the Best of Now and Here

No longer forward nor behind

I look in hope or fear;

But, grateful, take the good I find,

The best of now and here.

—John Greenleaf Whittier

Planting Jelly Beans

One Sunday when my daughter was two or three, a well-meaning nursery leader gave her a paper cup full of dirt, a small shriveled bean . . . and delusions of grandeur. Hilary stuck the pitiful little thing in the soil, watered it faithfully, and was rewarded in time with a sickly green beanstalk that couldn't have supported an aphid, let alone a giant-killer. Nevertheless, it was her first participation in the law of the harvest, and she was hooked.

Since that time, my little sower has strewn pumpkin seeds and popcorn, melon seeds and M&Ms, potatoes and potato bugs, with varying levels of success. She's planted with no regard to season, soil, or the anticipated crop—and she's been equally delighted with radishes and roses. Even when nothing at all comes up, she's content, because for her the satisfaction is in the sowing.

I want to be like that, but I tend to be crop-oriented. My first calling as a Young Women president was in a ward where one of the Laurels wanted nothing to do with the Church. I considered that girl's conversion and eventual exaltation my personal responsibility. On the way to her house to introduce myself, I day-dreamed of the positive impression I would make, and of the *New Era* article she'd write about me. (You know the kind of story I mean: "Sister Incredible Touched My Heart: Generations Will Rise Up and Call Her Blessed.")

The only problem with my dream was that the girl didn't want to change her life, so I never touched her heart. I didn't even touch her *stomach,* since she refused every treat I ever offered. Once, she got up off the couch long enough to call me a couple of things, but "blessed" wasn't one of them. I sowed seeds of love and fellowship as faithfully as I could, but I reaped failure and discouragement. I might as well have planted one of Hilary's jelly beans under a rock in the blistering Arizona sun and expected to grow a bright, beautiful jelly beanstalk.

Everybody knows that planting jelly beans is fruit-less. Or is it?

About a year ago, I drove from my rural home into town—a smallish community in central Arizona. On the way, I listened to reports from Iraq about two

48

young soldiers who'd been captured by the enemy, brutally tortured, and mutilated after their deaths. With two sons of my own in uniform, I felt angry, heartbroken . . . and powerless to do anything but feel angry, heartbroken, and powerless. Downtown, crossing the courthouse plaza, I passed an old memorial to men who fought in World War II. I've passed that statue dozens of times without giving it a second glance, but that day I noted that several people had gathered around it and that more than one of them was sobbing. Curious, I walked over to look for myself. At the bronze soldiers' feet someone had placed two long-stemmed red roses wrapped in a black POW flag—a small, spontaneous tribute to two young servicemen, neither one of whom was from Arizona, who'd given their lives in a war-torn land half a world away.

I looked at the flag-wrapped flowers and thought about how similar that act was to planting jelly beans.

When I passed by again an hour later, another group had paused before the newly significant memorial. Few eyes were dry. I retrieved my camera from the car and took a picture, which I posted on a "military mom" website as soon as I got home. Within an hour, dozens of mothers with children in Iraq wrote to say how comforted and blessed they felt because someone cared so deeply about those two young soldiers—and thought to demonstrate their compassion. That simple, spontaneous gesture, like a single seed, bore more delicious fruit than its sower could ever have imagined.

I resolved that day to be less crop-oriented myself. It is now my habit to drop a jelly bean or two whenever and wherever I can. It's likely that most of my "magic beans" fall by the wayside or are trodden underfoot, unobserved and unappreciated. But maybe—just maybe—someday one will take root. In the meantime, I still keep an eye out for other people's jelly beanstalks. While they don't grow often, when they do they're incredibly bright and impossible to miss. In fact, if you look up high enough, you'll see that their tops do indeed brush heaven!

Please Pass the Geritol™

It has recently come to my attention that I am old. Not older than the hills or older than some of the jokes my husband tells at the dinner table, but old just the same. Since I still feel twenty, I might never have noticed the passage of the . . . ugh . . . *decades* if my class hadn't gotten together for a thirty-year high school reunion. (Think "Future Crypt Keepers of America," and you'll picture that evening perfectly.)

For the sake of the many of you who were toddling around the premortal existence when I graduated, I'll give you a quick review: 1976 was America's bicentennial. Gerald Ford was president, but not for long. Bicentennial aside, it had been an unremarkable decade. We'd been born a little too late for the Beatles and Vietnam, but a little too early for disco and Desert Storm. The Grammy-winning song in 1976 was "Love Will Keep Us Together" by Captain and Tennille, and the Emmy for best actress went to Lindsay Wagner for her role in *The Bionic Woman*. The first *Bionic Woman,* that is.

Believe it or not, we survived adolescence without microwave ovens, personal computers, the Internet, iPods, cell phones, CDs, DVDs, DVRs, LCDs, HDs, and even—*gasp*—VHS. (We thought eight-track tapes and Atari were the coolest things that would ever be invented.) It was still a "Brady Bunch" kind of world, notable for its awful fashion sense. We girls wore Gunny Sax to prom, escorted by boys in pastel-hued tuxedos. Male or female, we had big hair, big glasses, and big plans to change the world.

The world has changed a lot since then, but most of the people I know haven't been responsible for it.

One of my favorite authors, Janette Rallison, wrote an article in which she quoted James Fleck: "If religious-minded people can't use the media effectively then a-religious and antireligious people will form the value systems of the world." Janette then added, "I take that statement very seriously because I've seen it happen in my lifetime. I grew up watching *The Dick Van Dyke Show, The Andy Griffeth Show,* and *The Brady Bunch.* Do any of you remember when *Love Boat* was shocking? Well, TV has come a long way; so have books. This has sparked a debate: does media influence behavior, or does behavior influence media?"[11]

I think it's both. I also believe that we each have a greater responsibility to influence the media, without being influenced by it, than we now exercise. With the remarkable growth of the Church, it's now truly possible for LDS people to help shape the value system of the world. While most of us vote our conscience in the political arenas, do we do as well when it comes to voting with our dollars in the public sector? How often do we lower our standards when it comes to books, magazines, and television? When we can't find anything in the theater listings that is of good report and praiseworthy, do we stay home, or do we pay to see something that's "not too bad" or "really good, except for one or two parts"?

Having written that, I must also admit that I have too often fallen into the latter group. (I confess this because even if I don't yet qualify for the ranks of the saints, I'd like to at least stay off the rolls of the hypocrites.) The whole entertainment industry is truly one of the "flying monkeys" in my life. (And you'll just have to read on for an explanation of the term!) Admitting this gives me hope that if recognition is the

---

[11] Rallison, Janette, "Presidency Message," *Of Good Report* (Newsletter of the American Night Writers Association), July 2006, 1.

first step toward repentance, I am at least heading in the right direction!

As are most of us. The explosion of growth in LDS publishing and music, coupled with the emergence of a mostly well-supported LDS film industry, shows me that we're at least—and at last!—*trying* to influence the media for the better. I'm glad. And I want to do my part. Even though I'm indisputably old, I may yet have a few good years left. After all, President Hinckley is almost twice my age, and he's still building and blessing and saving the world one day (temple, general conference) at a time. Perhaps I'll have another "lifetime" left to devote to the cause—a life mostly free of diapers, PTA carnivals, and Little Leagues this time around. If that is true, how do I best invest it? As an author, a woman of principle, a Latter-day Saint, what should I—what should we—be doing in the next thirty or fifty or ten or two or however many years we have left in our turns on earth?

Hopefully you already know the answer, because I'm still working on it. Determining what to do with my life is third on my to-do list. I plan to get right on it just as soon as I've repented of my less-than-Pauline choices and found a terrific wrinkle cream and homeopathic remedy for hot flashes!

That Our Country Still Stands Is Payment Enough for Me and Mine

I have a sticker on the back of my car that says "Proud Parent of a US Marine." I stuck it there myself when my youngest son entered boot camp. For a long time I drove around town feeling like a liar. What I needed was a sticker that said "*Puzzled* Parent of a US Marine." Here was a kid who had every opportunity to go to college without the GI Bill. He had a good job, a good car, a comfortable room, a big-screen TV, and a surround-sound system that would do credit to a Cinemark theater. More importantly, he had a fairly functional family and terrific friends—a couple of whom were of the beautiful female variety. This he traded for the motto "Pain Is Weakness Leaving the Body," a platoon of smelly fellow-recruits, and a drill instructor with pointy teeth who could have benefitted from etiquette lessons from the Terminator. Most puzzling, he did it at a time when one or two or ten young Americans were dying each week on foreign soil. You know what? Forget puzzled. What I really needed was a sticker that said "*Petrified* Parent of a US Marine."

In Matt's second week of training, we received a letter from Robert C. Oaks that shifted my paradigm, at least a little. A former four-star general, Oaks is now a General Authority in the Church. He wrote, "In these troubled times, it is heartwarming to see sons and daughters courageously step forward to help preserve our freedom and way of life. You can be proud of the part you played in molding Matt's character. Courage and patriotism do not come automatically; they are planted in the hearts of children by their parents."

Excuse me? As much as I hate to pick a quarrel with a General Authority, the fact that I now have two sons serving in the military is *not* my fault. In fact, I suspect they have a genetic defect.

In the spring of 1777, their ancestor Philip Bonesteel turned his back on his nobleman heritage in England to enlist as a minuteman in fledgling New York. When the War of Independence drew to a close, he was twenty-two years old, homeless and penniless, but he was an American.

Fourscore and five years later, John Manche, an Indiana farmer, left his wife and two small children behind to serve in the Civil War. Later, desperately poor and still suffering from wounds received at Gettysburg, John received his first pension payment, along with a letter praising him for his courage on the field of battle. He sent the money back to Washington with a letter of his own that said, "A man does not offer his life for the honor of other men. A Christian does not take the life of a brother for silver or gold. I fought, sirs, to preserve my country. That she still stands united is payment enough for me and mine."

My dad was an ordinary high school kid when Pearl Harbor was bombed and America entered its second world war. He coerced his widowed mother to sign papers allowing him to enlist before he graduated from high school or turned eighteen. He fought in Guam and the Philippines and was aboard a carrier when it was torpedoed on the open sea. He served through the end of World War II and then fought in Korea, very near where my oldest son serves today. He was in the Navy for twenty-five years.

So, with all due respect to Elder Oaks, I blame those guys. Courage and patriotism do reside deep in my sons' hearts—as deep as they did in the hearts of their forefathers. Like Philip Bonesteel, they were determined to ignore the well-intentioned advice of parents and leave a comfortable home to enlist as freedom fighters. Like John Manche, they serve for the right reasons. (Although I do believe they cash their meager paychecks.) Like my father, they do their jobs wherever they are sent, knowing they could die in defense of their beliefs.

I've had that sticker I told you about on my car for more than three years now. While I'm still petrified, I'm no longer puzzled. I might even be proud. There have been a lot of veterans in my family, patriotic men who stepped forward during the worst of times in our country's history. How surprising should it be that there are two more in this generation?

Am I Off to See the Wizard This Way?

I have a pair of ruby slippers. (Okay, so they're glitter-covered plastic shoes, but they're red and shiny and very cool just the same.) I don't wear them to enrichment night or the grocery store, but I do keep them handy because, like Dorothy Gale, someday I'll want to go home.

I see *The Wizard of Oz*[12] as a metaphor for life. The people who populated L. Frank Baum's fantasy searched for the strength of character we all need to make it back to our heavenly home. The Scarecrow, for instance, needed a brain. Don't we all? For one thing, we need to be smart enough to stay on the yellow brick road instead of wandering off into orchards where we're likely to be pelted by bad apples. Prophets tend to call this avenue toward righteousness the strait

---

[12] Baum, L. Frank, *The Wonderful Wizard of Oz* (Chicago: George M. Hill, 1900).

and narrow path. Sure, it's less colorful, but definitely more to the point.

The Tin Man sought a heart. There's nothing more important for us to cultivate. President Hinckley said, "Love is the very essence of life. It is the pot of gold at the end of the rainbow. Yet it is more than the end of the rainbow. Love is at the beginning also, and from it springs the beauty that arches across the sky on a stormy day."[13] Love, then, is like the Polar Star—the one constant in an ever-changing world.

The Cowardly Lion sought courage. Me too. I do, after all, have twenty-four-hour access to CNN. The scriptures tell us that if we're prepared, we shall not fear. Are we? Prepared, I mean. To be prepared, we have to recognize in advance that there are things in Oz (and the world) to look out for. Remember that beautiful field of flowers? If you left the path to rest in the poppies for even a moment you lost all interest in who you were and where you were going and simply fell asleep. At the time Baum chronicled Dorothy's adventures in Oz, opium was the most pernicious drug in the world. Opium, as you probably know, is made from poppies. Baum warned his generation a century ago: stay away from poison poppies! That's even better advice today.

---

[13] Hinckley, Gordon B., "And the Greatest of These Is Love," *Ensign,* March 1984, 3.

Two more things about which Baum cautioned are wicked witches and flying monkeys. To me, the Wicked Witch represents occult and true evil—something most of us don't have too much trouble recognizing, avoiding, and even evaporating. It's those rotten flying monkeys that get us.

When I use the Oz metaphor in speaking to youth, I ask someone to come forward and hold a large picture of the Savior. Then I ask everyone in the room to concentrate on the picture for just fifteen seconds. All they have to do, I say, is focus on that picture and think about nothing else except Jesus Christ for fifteen seconds. Then I step a few feet away, wait two or three more seconds, then pull a stuffed monkey out of my bag. I activate a screeching voice box within it and toss it deep into the audience. Believe me, *everybody* looks away from the picture of Christ and at the "flying monkey." It's human nature.

Unfortunately, it is also within our too-human natures to be distracted by metaphorical flying monkeys as well. There are millions of them: television, movies, sports, work, the Internet, money, games, power, fame—whatever it is in the world that distracts us enough to take our eyes from the Savior, if only briefly.

I can go on. (And on, and on, and on—I'm like that.) But I'll only make one more comparison. The

Emerald City reminds me of the spacious building in Lehi's dream. It is bright and sparkling and beautiful on the outside, and it seems like it would be a whole lot of fun, but behind all that dazzle is nothing but sham. There's no power there. No promises. A few laughs, maybe, but no lasting joy. No wonder Dorothy toured the Emerald City and still wanted to go home.

And here's the funny thing about that: Despite what she thought, despite her fears and struggles and insecurities, the little farm girl from Kansas had within herself the ability to fulfill her destiny all along. When she'd successfully completed her mission, going home turned out to be the easy part. And thus it can be with us. No power on Oz—or earth—is stronger than our power to pray, repent, persevere, and progress. If we have faith in the plan, stick together, and stay on the strait and narrow yellow brick road, there's nowhere to go but home.

The ruby slippers are just a fashion statement.

The Birdwomen of Arizona

The Birdman of Alcatraz was a convicted killer who turned his life around by devoting his years behind bars to the care and study of birds. I suspect that if my mother were to compile a list of people she admires, Robert Stroud would be on it—probably after St. Francis of Assisi and John James Audubon, but possibly before Mother Teresa and people of lesser accomplishment like, say, Thomas Edison.

Frankly, my mother has gone to the birds.

I'd never have believed it if I hadn't seen it for myself. When my grandmother lived with us, her greatest joy was feeding the wild birds that flocked to our back door. My mother hated those birds, and with good reason. She bought a bright, shiny new car every few years; the birds left poop stains on the paint jobs. She took great pride in her carefully manicured yard; the birds scattered unsightly seed that grew into weeds and attracted bugs and vermin. Despite my mother's constant complaints about her fine-feathered enemies, *her* mother slipped me money every Saturday to ride my bike to the store for a ten-pound bag of seed. This went on for years. When Grandma succumbed to lung cancer, I worried that dozens of seed-deprived sparrows would follow their benefactor in a great migration toward the Light.

Years passed and my mother moved in with me. She'd sold her house and virtually everything she possessed. It's not much of an exaggeration to say that she arrived with her clothing, a chair, a bed, and a table. Oh, and one thing more: We were still assembling her bed when she handed me a ten-pound bag of birdseed and a cheap plastic birdfeeder, clearly left over from the Grandma administration. She said, "I hope you have a post for this."

I didn't, but the local lumberyard sold me one.

Five years have passed since then, and my mother—who has never been one for doing anything halfway—has eighteen birdfeeders and two birdbaths within view from her picture window. (But she is in town today, so there may be three birdbaths and twenty feeders before I finish writing this.) She caters to finches, sparrows, mourning doves, orioles, hummingbirds, and other winged creatures that I'd have to get out her bird book and binoculars to identify. By association, and much to her chagrin, she also feeds four squirrels, two hawks, a family of roadrunners, countless mice, and at least one fat king snake . . . not to mention most of the neighborhood cats. This circle of life she has going is not exactly convenient. (Except for the cats.) One example from many:

Before my son left for Iraq, he draped a Marine Corps–issued dress coat over his chin-up bar on the back porch. Before I could take it to the cleaners as I'd promised, an industrious oriole built a nest in one pocket and filled said nest with eggs. So as not to disturb the nursery—and get our eyes pecked out by the mother bird—we not only never got the coat cleaned, but we can no longer open the door leading to the back porch, nor can we turn on the porch light. This means that the cat has to be let in and out a window, and that I have to walk a half-mile around the house to feed the chickens and/or retrieve food from the freezer. But one must have priorities, and my mother's "priorities" are nesting.

Yesterday evening I looked out the window to see my mother sitting on the bench we put up when the fifteen-foot trek from the seed barrels to the feeders became too much for her to undertake without rest. A hummingbird hovered over her head, two doves pecked the ground near her feet, an oriole hung upside down from its nectar feeder nearby, and the St. Francis statue was knee-deep in sparrows. There sat the former bird-hater, looking as much a part of the scene as the bird-loving cement saint. The feathered fauna are so accustomed to her by now that the mechanical click of her oxygen tank no longer startles them, nor does the deep, rattling cough that often comes with her continuous struggle for breath.

I thought of how like the famed Birdman she is. In her case, the person she killed was herself. The weapon? Cigarettes. She is now serving, like her mother before her, a life sentence without possibility of parole. If she could take back the life-destroying choice she made as a young adult, she would. Because she can't, she's made another choice: to avoid despair and hopelessness by looking beyond her bodily prison. I wish you could see her gazing peacefully up into the sky, because it is yet another witness that He who marks the life of each sparrow knows and loves each of us so well. I think it was He who opened my mother's eyes to her mother's great love. Or perhaps He merely provided beautiful, hungry birds, and her boundless charity did the rest.

True confession: I don't love birds the way my grandmother did and my mother does. They're too messy and noisy and prolific and viciously territorial to elicit much of my admiration or affection. Nevertheless, it won't surprise me if the day comes when I arrive at my daughter's home with a suitcase in one hand and a beat-up plastic birdfeeder in the other.

She won't have a post, of course . . . but she'll get one.

The Bifurcating Badger Tree

I've been telling stories since I was old enough to lisp, "I saw a wabbit on Wocking Chaiw Woad!" but I learned to write stories by accident.

Rather, I learned to write because the counselors at my high school filled class schedules alphabetically. By the time they got to me, Blacks, Bellons, and Blairs occupied all the desks in the good classes, leaving us Wolfes, Wilsons, and Wellses with a choice of journalism or home ec. I didn't want to learn to report any more than I wanted to learn to rip seams or whip eggs. (I like to *make up* stories, remember? Even then I knew that fiction is frowned upon in journalism—unless, of course, you're a Pulitzer Prize–winning columnist or a presidential press secretary.) But since sewing machines are scarier than typewriters (have you seen those needles?), I took journalism.

This put me in Room 402, where the *Badger* was produced. The staff of the school newspaper was instructed and advised by first-year teacher Marv Abrams, also known as MEA, an enthusiastic, idealistic, left-wing liberal. (This in comparison to the rest of the population of Smallville, Arizona, where we lived.) The man didn't even speak English as we knew it. "This," he said, pointing to a diagram on the chalkboard, "is a bifurcating *Badger* tree."

I looked down at my spiral notebook but didn't take notes. I didn't know what "bifurcating" meant, but it sounded distasteful, possibly obscene.

"You will develop a strong sense of political efficacy!" he declared. I closed the notebook. I already had zits; I didn't need a bad case of efficawho on top of them. As soon as class ended, I practically ran down the hall to the counselor's office. Even basting seams and/or turkey carcasses was preferable to bifurcating efficacy everywhere.

But I never made the transition from Lois Lane to Suzie Homemaker. (If you don't believe me, ask my husband. He saw me at a computer just this morning, but he probably can't remember the last time he saw me at a stove.) I stayed in journalism because

(A) As I talked to the counselor, I remembered that I love words and that the man whose class I'd just fled seemed to know an impressively excessive number of them; and

(B) Home ec was full.

I went back to my seat in Room 402 . . . and stayed in it for three years.

Turns out I learned a lot of useful stuff along the way to graduation. In the word "fulfill" the fill is full. Philip pines for the Philippines. (Get it?) I could spell and pronounce "Caribbean" decades before *Pirates* came along to educate the rest of the world. I can also pronounce "ayatollah," but its spelling is a little iffy to me. (Or not. According to my spell-check, I nailed it on the first try!) Admittedly, the Philippines, the Caribbean, and ayatollahs were as difficult to work into a high school newspaper as they have been to use in LDS romance novels set in Arizona, so maybe learning to proofread backwards was more efficacious. For sure, learning to communicate on paper was one of the greatest blessings granted me in mortality.

So, while I may not have learned everything I needed to know in high school journalism, what I really needed to know (aside from how wrong it is to begin a sentence with a conjunction) is that enthusiasm and idealism are contagious. Tree-hugging aside, MEA was the first person I'd ever met who deeply cared—about his work, about the world, about "his" kids. By graduation, I still didn't want to become a journalist, but I did want to become a passionate, devoted world-mover like Mr. Abrams.

There are two points I want to make here. The first is that if there is a more Herculean or heroic job in the world than teaching, I don't know what it is. Thank goodness for those who undertake the education of America every day. Thank God (daily, in your prayers) for the gifted, gutsy few who do it with talent, passion, and devotion. They, more than the politicians, celebrities, and even religious leaders of our time, shape our future. I salute them.

But this essay isn't a tribute to them—or even to a loquacious, luminous pedagogue like MEA. At least, it isn't only that. It is a rumination about how God sometimes directs our footsteps down paths we'd rather not tread for reasons that might not become apparent for days, weeks, months, or even years.

Once, in my youth, I took a road that led toward a bifurcating *Badger* tree. That road, as Robert Frost would tell you, *has* made all the difference.

How Lo Do You Have to Go Before You Move a Mountain?

I have shelves lined with tomes of Tolstoy, Faulkner, Ibsen, Hardy, Longfellow, and other notable men and women of letters, but sometimes when I need great wisdom in just a few pages, I reach a little lower—to my collection of children's literature on the bottom shelves. Yesterday I reread *Ming Lo Moves the Mountain*.[14]

Arnold Lobel, who is probably best remembered for his Caldecott Honor books about Frog and Toad, also retold an ancient Chinese fable about a poor farmer who lived at the foot of a very large mountain. The mountain always cast a dark shadow, so the flowers and vegetables in Ming Lo's garden were very sparse. Clouds formed atop the cliffs, and heavy rain fell almost every day. Worst of all, rocks broke loose

---

[14] Lobel, Arnold, *Ming Lo Moves the Mountain* (New York: Greenwillow Books, 1982).

and fell on the heads of the hapless Ming Lo and his thoroughly disgruntled wife.

The wife insists that they can never be happy until Ming Lo moves that mountain, so he cuts down the tallest, thickest tree he can find and uses it as a battering ram. The tree splits in half, and Ming Lo falls on his head. The mountain does not move. Next, he beats pots and pans together, trying to make a noise loud enough to frighten the mountain away. The mountain does not move. He implores the gods to move the mountain for him. Either Ming Lo petitions the wrong gods or he lacks the faith of the brother of Jared, because still nothing happens.

At last the village wise man suggests one last course of action. He instructs Ming Lo and his wife to take their home apart, stick by stick, and gather together all their possessions. With these bundles on their backs, they must then do the "Dance of the Moving Mountain." It goes like this: Facing the mountain with your eyes closed, "you will put your left foot in a place that is in back of your right foot. Then you will put your right foot in a place that is in back of your left foot." This dance, the wise man says, must be done for many hours before success can be hoped for.

Hopeful (or perhaps desperate), Ming Lo and his wife gather up their meager possessions and begin to move their feet to the steps of the dance. After many hours, they open their eyes and can't believe what they see. They are under an open sky with a warm sun shining above. There are no falling rocks or storm clouds in sight. "Look," cries Ming Lo, "our dance has done its work! The mountain has moved away!"

Some people might interpret this story as a fable about a feeble-thinker, and, indeed, many Chinese folk stories share this theme. But I think Lobel meant to retell a powerful tale about perspective. Admittedly, I might think this because I have a lot of feeble-thinking Ming Lo in me. For some months now, I've lived at the base of the very tall, very dark Mt. Rushtowritenomore. Although I had a book released in 2007, I wrote it early in 2006. Since then I've written nothing at all. In the meantime, possibly everybody I know has rushed past me to conquer that pesky mountain. They've published a book, sold a book to a publisher, sent a newly completed book in, or started a tale that is sure to become their opus. While I'm genuinely thrilled for their skill and success as I watch them climb, they do tend to inadvertently knock a lot of rocks down on my head.

All this time I've been very proactive. Not. I've beat my fists against the mountain. I've talked a lot about it. I've even prayed for a miracle of the metaphorical geologic variety. Nothing's changed. I'm sure I'm asking the right God, I'm just not sure I'm asking for the right thing at the right time, and there's the rub. In the end, the mountain only seemed larger and darker and rockier than ever. Hopeless, in other words. I was so Ming Low I could barely open a laptop without being reduced to tears. I mean, a writer is a person who writes, right? So, since I can't (don't? won't?) write, I'm not a writer, right? And if I'm not a writer, then what am I? Tired of feeling like a sham, I finally told a friend about my woes. Being a wise woman, she said exactly the right thing: It was time for me to gather up my meager talents and do the "Dance of the Moving Mountain."

Truly, discouragement and despair and hopelessness often do come from the way we look at a thing. The more I looked at writing as a way to define myself and measure my worth, the bigger and darker and scarier the mountain became. The more I compared myself with others, the more rocks hit me squarely between the eyes. The more I railed and moped and beat myself up about everything I hadn't done or couldn't do, the darker the storm clouds became. But it wasn't hopeless. It's *never* hopeless when we finally remember to close our eyes long enough to take a step back from a difficulty. Any difficulty. If we put our right foot in a place that is behind our left foot and then our left foot in a place that is behind our right, we will eventually find that our mountains—while still looming large—will at last begin to come into perspective.

It's sunnier in the place I live today. The storm clouds are thinner here, so there are only scattered showers. I can still see my friends climbing the far peaks, of course, but without the rocks raining down on my head, I feel much more inclined to wave enthusiastically as I marvel at their success. Perhaps someday I'll climb the mountain again myself. But even if I don't, one thing is certain: I will never again set up camp at the base of it. Instead, I'll just keep doing the dance as long as it takes to keep that mountain of discouragement right where it belongs!

I Like MS Better When
It Stands for Manuscript

If I had back every dish I've dropped and broken in the last decade, I could invite Wyoming over for a sit-down dinner. (I chose a sparsely populated state so you wouldn't think I'm exaggerating.) I'm too stubborn to switch to paper dinnerware, but if Mikasa ever introduces a line of Blue Willow in rubberware, I'll be first in line at Dillard's.

Breaking dishes isn't the only thing I do routinely. I also trip over things left carelessly lying around the house—like loose threads and pet dander. I type "yrkerl" in an e-mail or a manuscript and don't notice that the word is Martian until somebody points it out to me. I say things like, "Someday, you'll go to the aardvark to make sacred covenants."

I wish I were making that last one up, but I'm not. I also wish I hadn't been speaking to a group of Young Women at the time, but I was. No, I wasn't touting a new anthropomorphic religion; it was just a random word my brain sent to my mouth when my heart was thinking "temple." All things considered, it could have been worse.

I do all this—and worse—because I have multiple sclerosis. It's a disease that's all in my head. No, really. It is. Little lesions, which in my case are on the upper part of my spinal cord, wreak havoc with the neurological signals my mind sends to various and sundry parts of my body.

I think "temple" and say "aardvark." I step on a piece of glass and don't know I've cut my foot until I see a trail of bloody footprints across the carpet. I tell a sister in my ward at ten in the morning that of course I can drive her to the doctor at eleven, but by 10:03 I've forgotten that she called. (That sister still isn't speaking to me, by the way.)

The memory thing, or lack thereof, is probably the worst. While I can remember how fast Aquaman swims (100 mph), I often can't remember the names of my four children. (Scott, Jake, Matt, and, um, Edgar. No, Edgar's the turtle. Amy. Or is that the chicken? Give me a minute. It will come to me. I've known that girl for twenty years now.)

Or maybe the worst is to never know until I wake up in the morning what the symptom du jour will be. Will I be able to walk? See? Understand the words on my computer monitor? Pick up the salt shaker by the third try? MS isn't a fun affliction exactly, but it is endlessly interesting.

I can scarcely believe I'm sharing this today with anybody with ten bucks to plop down on a book and a rudimentary understanding of the English language. Mostly, I'm still in denial. For sure I don't enjoy letting anybody outside my family know I have MS. Part of this is pride, of course, but part is self-preservation. You wouldn't believe how many "cures" there are out there for an incurable disease—aside from the treatment my neurologist recommends, I mean. His involves needles. Stuck in my stomach. Every day. *Ick.*

According to one friend, all I really have to do is drink Perky Potion. It's an amazing concoction of vitamins, minerals, papaya juice, and shoe polish that you can get for a mere $150 an ounce and, in my case, keep down for about three minutes. As bad as it is, I do prefer it to the miracle remedy offered by a former home teacher. This guy insisted that two dozen bee stings a day for sixteen weeks would fix me right up.

Gee, as fun as that sounds, I think I'll stick with my neurologist. At least his way involves only one sting—and no insects.

I've heard lots more ideas, but I'm running out of pages and I suspect you're running out of attention span.

What brought this to mind was a conversation I had at church last week with a wonderful guy who's at about the same place I am in the progression of the disease. We compared notes and, frankly, teared up a little because we're both getting worse than we ever thought we would.

He said, "You know, one day last week I couldn't remember the name of our cat."

I said, "I got in the car, drove into town, then couldn't remember what I'd gone there for." I haven't told my husband this, by the way. Good thing he doesn't read "women's books" or he'd take away my car keys. You are hereby sworn to secrecy.

The point is that by the end of the conversation we were both laughing so hard our sides would have hurt, except that our nerves misfire so badly that my right toe hurt and his left elbow itched. It's a better week because of him. A better life even. Sure, I still forget things. I still break things—and one of these days that "thing" will probably be my neck—but I still laugh at those things too.

I admire Teri Garr for saying, "Sure I have MS, but I have lots of other things too."[15] So do I. One of the things I have the most of is hope. Someday maybe I will walk into my aardvark's office and he'll have a real cow . . . I mean cure. In the meantime, I just have to

---

[15] Garr, Teri, Interview with CNN, broadcast Oct. 9, 2002.

remember to buy more dishes the next time I'm in town with my daughter . . . Whatshername.

Part III: Counting on the Promises

Whate'er we leave to God,
God does and blesses us.

—Henry David Thoreau, 1847

Why I Keep My
Worries in a Box

If you believe that feeling bad or worrying long enough will change a past or future event, then you are residing on another planet with a different reality system.
—*William James*[16]

I may, in fact, be queen of that planet William James was talking about. Over the course of my life I have worried about virtually anything and everything there is to fret over. I vividly remember being four years old and lying in bed at night, begging God to keep coyotes from jumping in the window to eat me up. No, I'd never known anybody who'd been bitten by a coyote, let alone eaten by one. I'd never even *seen* a coyote, but I worried just the same.

---

[16] James, William, *The Letters of William James,* ed. Henry James (Boston: The Atlantic Monthly Press, 1920), 1:193.

By the time I was a teenager I'd mostly stopped worrying about coyotes—but only because I was now obsessed with (in no particular order): zits, nuclear war, making a C or better in geometry, dwindling global resources, prom, children starving in Africa, obtaining a scholarship, plane crashes, hurricanes, volcanoes, sick kittens, contracting malaria. . . . You know, this list could go on indefinitely. If it headlined the news, was discussed in the lunchroom, or was mentioned *anywhere* in passing, I worried about it.

When I was in my early twenties, a television show called *Quincy* almost sent me over the edge. Every week, Jack Klugman offered something new and horrific over which to despair. Anthrax. Mad Cow Disease. Plague. My hands shook as I turned off the TV, and I went to bed feeling certain everybody I knew would soon die horribly of the malady du jour. After a particularly graphic episode on botulism I swore off canned foods for eight months.

The sad truth is, you name it and I've probably worried about it.

It was my grandmother who finally got me to abdicate my crown to the "Planet of the Worriers" and immigrate to Earth. She lived here, and she was the sanest, healthiest, happiest person I have ever known.

Her secret? She kept all her worries in a box.

No, really, she did! She had a wooden recipe box with this quote from Hugh Blair on the cover: "Worry not about the possible troubles of the future; for if they come, you are but anticipating and adding to their weight; and if they do not come, your worry is useless; and in either case it is weak and vain, and a distrust of God's providence."[17]

It took study and prayer for me to finally understand how worry is "a distrust of God's providence," but I understood the concept of a worry box the first time my grandmother showed it to me.

My grandmother had been widowed three times—the first in the midst of the Great Depression, when she was left almost penniless with two little boys to feed and clothe. She learned then that she could not possibly function and worry at the same time, so she wrote down all her worries, put them in a wooden recipe box, put the box away where she couldn't see it, and then spent twenty-three worry-free hours each day coping as best she could. In the twenty-fourth hour she opened the worry box, cried, and sometimes despaired.

But mostly she prayed.

She said that at the end of the hour, when she shut the box, she could always go to sleep, because she knew that while the worries themselves may not have

---

[17] Blair, Hugh, *Lectures on Rhetoric and Belles Lettres* (Edinburgh: University of Edinburgh, 1783).

passed, the time to obsess over them had. She simply left them in God's hands and went to bed.

Somehow He always managed to handle the things she couldn't.

My grandmother has passed on and left me in a world where there are still earthquakes and famine and rumors of war and sick kittens and botulism and even—believe it or not!—coyotes on the back roads of Chino Valley. But those are the least of the worries I keep in my box. I now have elderly, often-ailing parents; an incurable, debilitating disease; a daughter with an ovarian cancer scare; and two sons in the military— one a Marine in Iraq. Since nobody in my situation could help but worry, I faithfully write it all down to be attended to promptly at three o'clock every afternoon. Except on weekends. Or Tuesdays when I have Cub Scouts . . . or days when I'm distracted by driving some- body to a doctor's appointment . . . or Fridays when I'm too busy cleaning out all my mother's bird feeders . . . or, well . . . sometimes I just forget altogether.

And that's okay. I know it won't surprise you to hear that the God of my grandmothers has never failed me either. As my faith increases, my worry decreases, and so there are days when I forget to open my little Pandora's Box of troubles at all.

But, believe me, I'd have never left "home" without it!

So, What's News?

Do you ever sit at your computer, staring at the headlines and wondering what we're doing in this handbasket and where we might be headed? I do it a lot more than I really should. Worse, I tend to provide my own personal commentary on most of the stories. Case in point from a single morning, chosen at random:

Associated Press: By midmorning, the mercury was at 90 in New York City, 92 in Philadelphia and Boston, and 97 in Richmond. . . . With the humidity, temperatures felt like 100 or higher.

Me: Excuse my callousness, but in Phoenix we call 100-degree weather *winter*. If it's not hot enough to fry a rattlesnake egg on the sidewalk (above 110) or melt the asphalt at the airport (above 120), it's not hot. If heat were the serial killer some of these reporters claim, there'd be approximately four million fewer people in southern Arizona. What most often kills people in heat waves is stupidity. They drink beer or cola instead of water and wonder why they dehydrate. A little knowledge and preparation would go a long way toward solving the problem.

(Note to self: There is a lesson for you in that "be prepared" advice. While you may indeed have plenty of water and six or eight 72-hours kits, at least one of those kits is stocked with formula and diapers. The baby recently turned twenty. You'd better get up from the computer and work on that. Well, maybe after the next story. . . .)

Associated Press: "I've spoken to the bear's owner, and he is not very pleased at all." —Daniel Medley, manager of a museum where a $75,000 teddy bear was ripped apart by the overnight guard dog.

Me: My dog dreams of things like that! While I frequent thrift stores to keep her supplied with stuffed toys to maul, I'd never pay seventy-five cents—let alone $75,000—for a bear. A $75,000 fuzzy? Wow. Some people have way too much disposable income. I wish I were one of them. What would I do with it, you ask? Probably update my 72-hour kit and buy a ten-year supply of fuzzies for my dog. Everything left over (which would be most of it) I would give to charity. My grandmother (the one who kept her worries in a box) used to say that if all your problems could be solved by money, you didn't have any problems.

Associated Press: "Shiite and Sunni are going to have to love their children more than they hate each other." —General Peter Pace, chairman of the Joint Chiefs of Staff, testifying before Congress on what must happen before there will be peace in Iraq.

Me: Marine generals generally aren't renowned for their philosophic bents, but this statement strikes me as profound. I wish soldiers and Marines all over the world could lay down their guns and put up billboards that say, "Can't we all just love our children more than we hate our neighbors?"

If that sounded sardonic, I didn't mean for it to. I think there's eternal truth in what General Pace said. Of course the signs would have to be printed in Arabic. And Hebrew. And Arabic again (for Hezbollah). And Korean. And Dari Persian. And English. And . . . how many languages are there in the world, anyway? At any rate, I love the thought and I like the man better for having said it.

That's it for me today. What's news in your part of the world?

How the Chess Champion Met His Match . . . I Mean Mate

My husband never had a chance.

Gary and I attended the same high school back when there were three billion fewer people in the world. I know this fascinating census tidbit because "population explosion" was the "inconvenient truth" of the 1970s. The dinosaurs had recently become extinct, and some scientists—or were they politicians?—predicted we humans would be next if we didn't stop multiplying and replenishing. Nevertheless, people all over the earth continued to throw caution to the wind, stubbornly marrying and being given in marriage despite the dire warnings of disaster-to-come. This, of course, brings me to the thesis of this essay: courtship and marriage.

As I was about to say before I was distracted by population explosion/global warming, I knew Gary

Blair in high school. He was quite frankly the stereo-typical boy-next-door. If you've ever seen *Happy Days,* think Richie Cunningham and you'll have Gary pegged. Since I had a thing for Ron Howard way back in the Opie Era, I might have thrown myself at Gary a half-decade sooner except for three things:

- He was president of the . . . *shiver* . . . chess club.
- He was . . . *shudder* . . . LDS. (Unlike my great-aunt, I didn't truly believe Mormons had cloven hooves under their gym socks, but I did believe they were kind of cliquish and maybe a little holier-than-thou.)
- I was already going with a guy.

The guy I was going with was more like the Fonz—minus the leather jacket, the motorcycle, and modesty. Still, he was handsome, smart, and funny (in a cynical, acerbic kind of way), and he drove a great car. What more could one want in a future mate? Besides, marriage wasn't a big deal. You got married if you happened to feel like it, and you kept the mate as long as it was still fun and/or convenient. ("The Family: A Proclamation to the World" had not yet been written; and if it had been, my family wouldn't have owned a copy.)

Then it happened. Two know-it-alls in white shirts and conservative ties came along, and the next thing thing I knew, marriage wasn't something that lasted until you turned thirty. Heck, it didn't even end at death. It went on forever. (And ever. And ever.) Although I tried to hang in with my boyfriend, I soon began to realize that my steady and I went together about as well as oil and water. Remember me telling you that Mormons are cliquish? Well, I think it must have something to do with the font water. Anyway, contemplating home and family—and that simply terrifying eternity clause—I knew that since I'd added the waters of baptism to my life, if I wanted to mix with oil it had better be of the consecrated variety.

About that time, Gary came home from a mission. Since I was now in the clique (and a natural when it came to holier-than-thou attitudes), he asked me out. We dated a couple of times and then worked together running stage lighting for summer events at the fairgrounds. Gary was just as cute and wholesome as ever, but he was also something more. He was a righteous man of God whom I admired tremendously. I hadn't, however, broken up with my longtime boyfriend for good. (All kinds of good, as it turned out.) In fact, on the last night Gary and I were to work together, I'd spent the day with the other guy. As usual, we debated marriage. When he finally dropped me off at the fairgrounds, Gary was just getting out of his car across the lot. My boyfriend sarcastically said, "If you really want everything you say you do, why don't you marry Gary Blair?"

I slammed the door hard enough to rattle his teeth and yelled, "You know what? I think I will!"

I did, in fact. Ten months later (it took Gary that long to admit that resistance was futile), we were married for time and all eternity in the Mesa Temple. Since the sealer assured us that earth-replenishing was still a good thing, we did that too.

I told you the poor guy never had a chance.

True Love Is Like a Ghost

The tagline of my second Nightshade novel, *Ghost of a Chance,* is "True love is like a ghost. Many people believe in both, but few find either." It's an updated version of a line written by a guy named Francois de la Rochefoucald (see why I didn't just quote him?) in 1789: "True love is like a ghost; everyone talks of it, but few have met it face to face."

However you put it, I believe it.

For the record, I do not drag my husband to cemeteries to hunt for ghosts. We went to the cemetery because I thought a graveyard would be a unique place to take a picture for my website, and the old Citizen's Cemetery in my hometown has long been one of my favorites.

Everybody has a favorite graveyard, right?

Buried therein are the remains of men who served as Rough Riders with Teddy Roosevelt, and women who served . . . um, something . . . in the Bird Cage saloon on Whiskey Row back when Doc Holladay used to drop in.

It was a great place for a photo shoot. Unfortunately, the cemetery's high, wrought-iron gates are closed and locked at dusk. In order to get in, we had to park in one of the less-desirable parts of town and ignore the drunken party going on nearby. We said a quick prayer that our hubcaps—and the car to which they were attached—would still be there when we returned, and then we lowered ourselves over a rock wall and into the graveyard. Thanks to the miracle of gravity, this wasn't too difficult, even for a pudgy, middle-aged novelist and her CPA husband.

For about an hour, I led my eternal companion from one old sepulchre to the next (and the next and the next and the next) in search of the perfect spot in which to be photographed. While I graciously carried the compact digital camera, he carried my fifty-pound antique typewriter. The evening was cold, dark, and suitably spooky, even for me.

By the time we had enough pictures to make me happy, we'd attracted the attention of several drunks and one police officer—but no ghosts. (Darn it.) My husband boosted me back over the wall, handed up the typewriter, considered the wall's height and his high blood pressure, and then sat down to wait for the cemetery's gate to open or for heaven's trump to sound, whichever came first.

No. Seriously, he scaled a crumbling pile of rocks and loose mortar that would have given Spider-Man second thoughts.

I probably don't have to tell you that Gary would have rather been home watching football and rooting for ASU that night. (In fact, he'd have rather been at a dentist's office having a root canal.) Nor do I need to tell you that I've found true love. You can see that for yourself.

Freaky Friday

Today is Friday the thirteenth. Fortunately, I am not superstitious. I know perfectly well that while this morning began with a series of unfortunate events, they have nothing whatsoever to do with the day or date. Here's what's happened thus far.

While I was sleeping, the cat deposited a hairball (super-deluxe, extra-slimy edition) on the exact spot on the floor my bare foot hits when I get out of bed in the morning. My shrill cry of dismay activated our biological alarm system (the pit bull), which barked loud enough to wake the neighbors up the street—the ones trying to get a little shut-eye in the cemetery.

After deactivating the dog and demucking my foot, I searched for my glasses. No luck. Thus I stumbled toward the bathroom like a newborn field mouse. Oh, wait. Bad analogy. There is a full-grown field mouse (or possibly a gigantic rat) decomposing at its leisure within the walls of my bathroom. The smell takes "putrid" and ratches it up six notches. When you read *Ghost of a Chance*—and I know you will—you'll come across a description of the odor of rotting flesh. Remember then that I know whereof I write.

When my stomach settled, I was ready for breakfast. Unable to make out the timer on the toaster oven (see "lost glasses," above), I reduced a blueberry bagel to a charcoal briquette. This wouldn't have been so bad if not for my new, high-tech smoke detectors.

"Smoke detected in kitchen!" a mechanical voice screeched hysterically. "Evacuate! Evacuate!" Before I could resume breathing, let alone turn off the alarm and/or run for my life, another took up the cry: "Smoke detected in hallway! Evacuate! Evacuate!" Soon, five hysterical voices were screaming all over the house. (Two of them were me and my mother.) I'd always wondered what happened to Will Robinson's robot when *Lost in Space* was cancelled. Now I know. He's doing voice-overs for a smoke detector manufacturer in Toledo. When that company starts adding little waving arms to their excitable, round boxes, they'll really have something.

If I were superstitious, I might attribute all this to the date on the calendar . . . or to the mirror I broke five and a half years ago, the ladder I walked under last week, or the black cat that crosses my path every time he musters up the energy to drag his fat, lazy carcass out of the easy chair. But I'm not superstitious. Really. I toss salt over my shoulder only because my grandmother did and it seems like a charming way to remember her. Everybody knocks on wood, picks up pennies, crosses their fingers, tosses coins into fountains, blows out candles on birthday cakes, and wishes on the first star of the evening, so none of that could be superstitious in origin. Right? Sure, I avoid stepping on cracks, but here in Arizona it's because they're likely to have centipedes in them. I hold my breath going through tunnels, but that's because I'm claustrophobic. Moreover, the horseshoe that hangs over my backdoor is a memento from a family camping trip. The European witching ball that hangs from the apple tree is a decoration, as is the Native American dream catcher over my mother's bed. The fairy rings on the front lawn form by themselves. (I can't grow a tomato, but if you ever need a poisonous toadstool for an omelet, I'm the girl to go to.) The four-leaf clovers in so many of my tomes are bookmarks. And, while I do sometimes remember to say "rabbit, rabbit" first thing on the first day of a month, I have never, ever possessed a rabbit's foot that was not still attached to a living, breathing bunny. (I currently have eight of those.)

So, clearly, I am not superstitious. So what if I just spilled orange juice on the keyboard, causing my right SHIFT key to stick? That could have happened on a Tuesday the tenth.

Don't worry, I'm fine, but I can't write any more today. In fact, I think I'll go back to bed. My throat feels a little scratchy. I may be coming down with something. Possibly paraskavedekatriaphobia. I hear it's going around.

Take Me Out to the Ball Game

The World Series begins tomorrow (October 20, 2006). At my house this means hot dogs for supper, peanuts and Cracker Jacks all around, and me and my mom glued to the television at five o'clock sharp, Mountain Standard Time. I am, you see, a fourth-generation baseball fan. Possibly a fanatic.

The baseball "defect" must be carried in the maternal genes. My grandmother bled Dodger-blue for almost ninety years. She was with me in the hospital for an October surgery in 1978. When I came to, the first thing she told me was the series standing and Orel Hershiser's ERA. She figured that since I'd lived, I'd want to know. (She was right.) Years later, when she was in the hospital dying of cancer, she wanted two things read to her religiously: the Psalms and the Dodgers' daily box scores.

Baseball has been here as long as America. A little longer, in fact. A soldier at Valley Forge wrote of General Washington, "He sometimes throws and catches a ball for hours with his aide-de-camp."[18] Every president has left at least one baseball-related story. This is my personal favorite: When informed of his nomination for president in 1860, Abraham Lincoln reportedly said, "I'm glad to hear of their coming, but they will have to wait a few minutes till I get my turn at bat."[19] Calvin Coolidge is credited with "officially" declaring baseball our national pastime, and Herbert Hoover wrote, "Next to religion, baseball has furnished a greater impact on American life than any other institution."[20]

My second-favorite presidential baseball story is about Ronald Reagan. In his broadcasting days, he was once announcing a game from a remote studio when the feed went dead. Without missing a beat, Reagan simply made up the next ten minutes' worth of plays. If anybody ever knew it, they didn't care. It's mostly how he ran our country, too, and we loved him for it.

But we're talking World Series. As you probably know, the St. Louis Cardinals take on the Detroit

---

[18] "Baseball Almanac," www.baseball-almanac.com, 2000–2007.

[19] Editorial Cartoon from 1860, "Baseball Almanac," www.baseball-almanac.com/prz_qal.shtml.

[20] "Baseball Almanac," www.baseball-almanac.com/qhh.shtml.

Tigers in the 2006 Fall Classic. Normally I'm National League loyal, but once in awhile I jump bleachers. I just had to root for the Red Sox a couple of years ago. This year I'm leaning toward the Tigers. Not only do I believe that people who eke out a living in Michigan should get *some* kind of prize for it once every quarter century or so, but the Tigers remind me of the 2001 Diamondbacks. Man, what a year! My only claim to baseball fame will probably always be that I published a book in June of that year (*The Heart Only Knows*) predicting that the new Arizona franchise would go to the World Series. When the D-Backs beat the legendary Yankees, my phone started ringing and didn't stop for three days. It was one of the highlights of my life . . . and I had nothing whatsoever to do with it!

That's the crazy thing about fanaticism. I can't quite remember the look on my husband's face when we knelt across the altar in the temple, and I've forgotten what the first kid they handed me in the labor-and-delivery room looked like, but I will always remember Jay Bell's face as he crossed home plate to win the 2001 World Series.

Let me tell you one great Tigers story, and then I promise to let you get on with *your* favorite pastimes. In 1934, the Tigers were playing for their first pennant since 1909—an eternity in baseball. They were led in both fielding and hitting by a young ballplayer by the name of Hank Greenberg, a Jew. Disaster struck when a decisive game fell on Yom Kippur, the Jewish Day of Atonement. Whether Hank would (or should) play on a holy day became a hotly debated issue across the country. He refused to enter the debate. He listened to his heart, made his decision, and stuck to it regardless of the consequences.

He went to temple instead of to the ballpark.

Edgar A. Guest immortalized it best:

Come Yom Kippur—holy fast day wide-world
  over to the Jew—
And Hank Greenberg to his teaching and the old
  tradition true
Spent the day among his people and he didn't
  come to play.
Said Murphy to Mulrooney, "We shall lose the
  game today!
We shall miss him on the infield and shall miss
  him at the bat,
But he's true to his religion—and we honor him
  for that!"[21]

The Tigers lost that day—but virtue won. One man stood up to be counted when it mattered most.

---

[21] Guest, Edgar A., *Detroit Free Press*, Sept. 12, 1934.

As baseball great Joe Garagiola wrote, "Baseball is only a game, but they keep a book on you. When it's all over for you, the game has got you measured."[22] This is precisely why I'll miss Sunday's game to go to church. But Monday and however many more days after that the series extends, I'm so there! As Yogi Berra said, "You can see a lot by just observing."[23]

I want to see it all!

---

[22] Garagiola, Joe Sr., *It's Anybody's Ballgame* (New York: Contemporary Books, 1988).

[23] Ibid; http://www.baseball-almanac.com/quotes/quoberra.shtml.

The Thousandth Time May Prove the Charm

Since my call as a Cub Scout den leader, I have become well-indoctrinated in the Law of the Pack. *The Cub Scout follows Akela. . . . The Cub Scout gives goodwill.* Got it. While I know the law and the promise and most of the handbook by heart, the eight-year-old boys I lead struggle to remember the motto: Do Your Best. If they were girls, they'd have not only memorized those three words, they'd have internalized them for life.

I don't know what it is about the female of the species—particularly the female of the LDS species—but "best" doesn't seem to be good enough. By the time we're adolescents, most of us think we should be perfect.

Why are we like that? Despite what some people may tell you, we *don't* learn it at church. Our leaders—

from the prophet on down—repeatedly counsel us to prioritize, simplify, and choose Mary-like lives over Martha ones. And yet we persevere in our craziness.

Maybe we just haven't heard the message enough times. In a little gem called *Mountain Interval*, Robert Frost wrote, "Our very life depends on everything's recurring till we answer from within. The thousandth time may prove the charm."[24]

Recently I stood on Temple Square in Salt Lake City, looking up at the temple and recalling in vivid detail when that "thousandth time" first struck me.

I was a new stake Relief Society president in an area that had recently endured a firestorm of controversy and hurt feelings. Under the stake president's direction, we planned an evening for the sisters designed to provide fellowship and healing. I wanted everything to be perfect. To make it so, my counselors and I worked feverishly for days, paying careful attention to every detail. Because harmony and beauty invite the Spirit, we'd color-coordinated the room decorations, the table coverings, and even the food. (Believe me when I say that everything was just peachy.)

One hour before the event, the only thing left to do was to set up the cake we'd ordered as the center-piece. My counselors went home to change clothes,

---

[24] Frost, Robert, "27. Snow," *Mountain Interval* (New York: Henry Holt, 1920), 31.

leaving me alone in a hall that was beautiful, peaceful, and completely quiet. As I opened the pastry box, a scream pierced the air.

I was the one screaming.

The cake was blue. Not pastel blue, or "just a little blue," or even robin-egg blue. It was Cub Scout blue-and-gold, uglier-than-sin blue. If it had been slathered with slime and adorned with live roaches, I couldn't have been more appalled. I knew then and there that unless I acted fast the whole evening would be ruined!

(You have to be an LDS woman—or possibly Martha Stewart—to understand that last paragraph.)

I ran home, grabbed all the white frosting and decorating bags I had in the cupboard (everybody has a year's supply of frosting, right?), and sped back to the church. I began to cry in frustration as I gripped the decorating bags in my teeth and balanced the tubs of frosting under one arm while struggling with the other hand to get the stupid magnetic key to activate the stupid green light that would give me 1.6 seconds to open the stupid glass door. I couldn't do it. The frosting, bags, key, and I all hit the concrete in the same moment. I'd had it. Let the evening go to the dogs. I was too tired and too stressed to care.

That's when I experienced one of the most meaningful lessons of my whole life. Through my tears I caught a glimpse of something bright and golden and shining. The setting sun had caused the letters firmly affixed to the side of the building to blaze as if on fire.

The Church of Jesus Christ of Latter-day Saints.

It must have been the thousandth time I'd seen His name on a Church building, because my heart really did answer from within. In fact, it pounded with such surety I could finally see the situation, and myself, rightly. I was trying with all my heart to do His will, but was I doing it in His way? What *would* Jesus do?

It was then that it occurred to me that while Christ had wept over those He loved, He certainly never shed a tear over a wrong-colored cake. Even the idea was absurd.

While I didn't see a vision, I did suddenly recall with vision-like clarity every story I'd read about Christ's mortal ministry. The Sermon on the Mount? No centerpieces there. No chairs, even. There were no linens or color-coordinated tableware when Christ broke bread with the Apostles. He hadn't offered sparkling punch to the woman at the well. He'd had no cake of any color to feed the five thousand. And yet everywhere Jesus Christ went there was living water and bread of life enough and to spare.

Then, because the Spirit knows me so well, it added, *Can you imagine Christ saying to His Apostles,*

"How does everything look? How did I do? Was it good enough? Do you think they liked me?"

It was a paradigm shift of eternal proportion.

While I had been planning and preparing and primping (and careful and troubled) about so very many things, I'd missed the one thing that was truly needful. I knew what I must do. Right there on the concrete outside the stake center door, I knelt beneath the glinting gold of those precious words and prayed. I asked in Christ's name for inspiration to know my sisters' needs. I begged to be able to offer the better part of myself as long as I lived to serve. I petitioned for forgiveness for being worldly and unwise when I'd meant to be so good—at least in my own eyes. I prayed that I might never, ever forget that "thousandth time" that I'd seen His name on "my" church and my heart had at last answered from within.

It was *then* that the true miracle occurred. My prayers were answered. And I have never been the same.

Romper, Stomper, Bomper, Boo!

Every September when the neighborhood kids go back to school, a part of me envies them. Another part, however, is thrilled to have those days behind me. It's not easy to always be a good Do Bee, you know.

I never got into trouble in school. I was one of only two people in class on Senior Ditch Day. And, yes, the other was the teacher. Let's face it: I was a teacher's pet worthy of a monogrammed collar and flea dip.

I blame Miss Nancy. Robert Fulghum claims to have learned everything he needed to know in kindergarten. Lucky guy. I was indoctrinated about life by *Romper Room*.

I'm here to tell you that what the television programs *Night Gallery, Dark Shadows,* and *Twilight Zone* were to adults, *Romper Room* was to us sixties-era preschoolers. I never missed it. In fact, I learned to tell time in the pre–digital-clock years (sometimes referred to as the Dark Ages) so I wouldn't be a minute late turning on the TV. Good Do Bees were never late to *Romper Room,* and I was so scared of the teacher, Miss Nancy, that I was undoubtedly the best Do Bee in fifty contiguous states.

The first thing we did each day was stand to recite the Pledge of Allegiance. I still put my left hand over my right lung because that's how I thought Miss Nancy did it. (Turns out televisions and mirrors are not exactly the same technology.) Next we sang the Do Bee Song. *Do be a Do Bee. Don't be a Don't Bee. . . .* The lyrics weren't much, and the melody wasn't catchy, but I sang it fervently. It was during this lesson that my core values were formed. Do Bees were turn-takers. Don't Bees were friend-shakers. (I only sang it; I can't explain it.) In short, Do Bees were trustworthy, loyal, helpful, friendly, courteous, kind, obedient, cheerful, thrifty, brave, clean, and reverent. (You only thought that was Boy Scouts. Lord Baden-Powell probably got the idea from Miss Nancy.) And Don't Bees? Well, there simply weren't any Don't Bees on *Romper Room.*

That was Terrifying Toddler Truth Number One: Good Do Bees who went bad "went away." I swear. Many days I sat with my pudgy little palms pressed to my cheeks, crying, "Be a Good Do Bee!" to Robbie or Jeffy or Johnny, little boys who insisted on taking an extra cookie or stomping around too enthusiastically on their Romper Stompers. (Romper Stompers were yellow plastic buckets with green nylon ropes attached. All the true-blue Do Bees owned at least one pair. I had two.) I almost fainted when a kid sassed Miss Nancy . . . and without raising his hand!

Saintly Teacher never scolded, but one side of her lips turned down while the opposite eyebrow rose. I knew what that meant, and I despaired. Sure enough, after the next commercial, Robbie or Jeffy or Johnny was gone, replaced without explanation by a Do Bee with no cowlick and better table manners. For years I've searched cornfields and studied the backs of milk cartons, hoping for a clue to what happened to all those little boys. Alas, only Miss Nancy knew, and she probably took the secret with her to her grave. (Let's hope that's all she took!)

As hard as it is to believe, I hated snack time. In the first place, the blessing on the cookies really bugged me. *"God is great. God is good. Let us thank Him for our food."* Excuse me, but even a Dumb Bee knows that good and food don't rhyme. In the second place—and speaking of bugging—my mother always bought oatmeal cookies with raisins. Everybody knows that raisins are dried fly carcasses. I ate them anyway, of course. That's what Do Bees did on *Romper Room,* because if Do Bees didn't, they were Don't Bees, and even homebound Don't Bees quailed before the second terrible truth.

Terrifying Toddler Truth Number Two was that you didn't have to be in the Romper Room itself for Miss Nancy to see you and send you away by remote! I'm not making this up. Miss Nancy possessed a mirror that was heck's cheap imitation of the Urim and Thummim. At the close of every show, she raised the horrific device, narrowed her eyes, and chanted this incantation: *"Romper, Stomper, Bomper, Boo! Tell me, tell me, tell me, do! Magic Mirror, tell me today: Did all our friends have fun at play?* Then began the appalling litany: *I see Stephanie. I see Julie. I see . . ."*

By the time she'd said "boo," I'd already scurried for cover under the table or behind the couch. There I crouched with the newspaper and two pillows over my head, praying that Miss Nancy wouldn't see me or, if she did, wouldn't discern that I watched *Romper Room* only out of mortal terror. Every time she'd say "Gary" or "Cheri" or similar near misses, I'd fall into a paroxysm of panic. That was silly, of course. Nobody was safe. Miss Nancy's last words to us were always *And I see you too!*

I believed that with all my impressionable, pounding little heart.

As a first school experience, *Romper Room* affected me profoundly. ("Scarred me for life" is another way of putting it.) I carried Miss Nancy's code with me to kindergarten and beyond. While I never actually saw a Don't Bee disappear from the public school system, I wasn't willing to take the chance. What if Miss Nancy and her ilk had advanced from magic mirrors to *Stepford* technology? I wouldn't put it past her, nor could I take the chance.

Although I'm long out of school, I'm still a very good Do Bee. I'd like to credit goodly parents and the gospel of Jesus Christ for keeping me on the straight and narrow path, but I suspect I owe much of it to Miss Nancy. For sure I still raise my hand, drink my milk, and pick up my toys. After all, I can only assume Teacher has retired. What if she's still out there? What if she's still sitting, pale and formidable, in a black-and-white Romper Room somewhere, squinting into her magic mirror and waiting for me to finally screw up?

"Without Them, There Will Be No Other Rights to Guard"

Did you know that America celebrates an annual Armed Forces Day? If you turn your calendar to May, you'll see it printed in the little square between Bank Holiday (UK) and Victoria Day (Canada). I'll bet you've never circled it. Nobody pays much attention to Armed Forces Day unless their loved one wears the uniform of one of those forces. I circle it every year. Twice. My oldest son is an Army medic recently home from Korea, and my youngest is a Marine MP, a two-time veteran of Iraq, currently serving in the Pacific. Indulge me then while I tell you why you should care about this day, and care deeply.

In May of 1950, Harry S Truman issued a presidential proclamation establishing the holiday and calling for "the celebration of that day in such manner as to honor the Armed Forces of the United States."[25] It was primarily designed to increase awareness, not so much of what the military does, but of who they are—sons, daughters, husbands, wives, parents, siblings—the real people wearing the helmets and flak vests in submarines, tanks, and cockpits.

On May 17, 1952, the *New York Times* noted, "This is the day on which we pay special tribute to all the individuals who are in the service of their country all over the world. It won't be a matter of parades and receptions for a good many of them. They will all be in the line of duty, and some of them may give their lives in that duty."[26]

Unfortunately, that's as true today as it was fifty-six years ago. Possibly more so. I belong to two online groups of military mothers who have banded together to try to support our children and each other as best we can. This month—which is barely half over—I have written nine condolence letters to mothers whose sons were killed in Iraq. Nine. The youngest Marine to die between Mother's Day and Armed Forces Day was nineteen. The oldest soldier was twenty-three. I wish I could say that this May has been a rare month, but what's rare is for three or four consecutive days to pass in which I *don't* write at least one letter to

[25] "A Tradition of Heroes: Armed Forces Day History," United States Department of Defense, www.pentagon.gov/afd/military/history.html.
[26] "A Tradition of Heroes: Armed Forces Day History."

someone whose child has given his or her life for our country.

Hearts must be very resilient things, or mine would have broken into a million pieces by now.

So isn't it indeed "fitting and proper," as President Dwight D. Eisenhower said, "to devote one day each year to paying special tribute to those whose constancy and courage constitute one of the bulwarks guarding the freedom of this nation and the peace of the free world"[27]? As President John F. Kennedy added so succinctly, "Word to the Nation: Guard zealously your right to serve in the Armed Forces, *for without them, there will be no other rights to guard.*"[28]

I am proud of my sons for their honor, courage, and commitment. They know the price they might be called to pay. They enlisted in time of war because they genuinely want to serve their country, preserve our freedom and safety, and become the best men they can be. I admire them, my father, my father-in-law, my uncles, and the thousands of men and women who are like them. I *will* remember them on Armed Forces Day—and always.

"These are the times that try men's souls," Thomas Paine said more than two centuries ago. "The summer

---

[27] Eisenhower, Dwight D., "Presidential Proclamation, 1953"; quoted in "A Tradition of Heroes: Armed Forces Day History."

[28] Kennedy, John F., "Armed Forces Day Address," May 1962; italics added; quoted in "A Tradition of Heroes: Armed Forces Day History."

soldier and the sunshine patriot will, in this crisis, shrink from the service of their country; but he that stands it now, deserves the love and thanks of man and woman."[29]

Amen.

---

[29] "A Tradition of Heroes: Armed Forces Day History."

Can You Believe It?

Do you ever wonder about passion? I'm not talking about the passion of Christ or the kind of passion mostly left out of LDS romance novels. I'm talking about the passion (fervor, ardor, zeal) that all children of God share—the passion to create. Most of us work at it every day, whether at a keyboard, at a drawing board, or in studios, kitchens, or classrooms around the world. I think the creative impulse is hardwired into our brains, so I don't wonder why we do it. I wonder why we create what we do. Is that where passion enters in?

As a writer, I've been counseled more than once to think more "mainstream" in my choice of characters and genres. In other words, to write for the market rather than follow around whatever oddball character interests me at the moment. I suspect I would be more successful if I followed this advice, but I don't think I'd be as happy. Besides, I'm not the only oddball creator around. For sure I'm not the oddest.

I recently visited one of the many Ripley's Believe It or Not! museums located around the globe. I love those places! After an obligatory glance at the macabre and sensational (shriveled heads and pictures of fat women don't interest me much since I have a mirror at home), I spent an hour or more marveling at the creations. In the center of the Texas museum is an intricate, twenty-four-foot high model of the Eiffel Tower constructed from 110,000 toothpicks and five gallons of glue. I must have stood there for ten minutes wondering who would create that model—and why.

It wasn't the most amazing thing I saw. There was an awe-inspiring picture of Christ that from a few steps away looked like a charcoal sketch. When you approached, it turned out to be the Gospel of John (yes, all of it) rendered in some of the world's tiniest calligraphy. How long did that take? Was its creator bored to desperation, possessed, or uniquely inspired?

And yet that wasn't the most unbelievable creation, either. The most awesome to me was a gorgeous, tremendously lifelike picture of an ocean liner. The artist was so skilled you could almost see the ship move through the water while the sun glinted off its bow and seagulls circled overhead. It could easily have taken center stage in a bona fide art museum. At least it could have if it hadn't been painted on the head of a pin. You had to look through a microscope to see this picture, and the plaque accompanying it said the artist had painted it using a single human hair. Who would do that? Who *could* do it? *Why* would he do it even though he could?

These are passions I don't understand and yet admire tremendously. Forget the roads less traveled; some creative souls forge paths through the wilderness! And isn't that a good thing? If your passion leads you off the well-trod paths of conventional art or literature, shouldn't you go for it?

Believe it or not (I had to work that in somewhere, and I'm running out of letter), nobody had ever written a novel before Murasaki Shikibu penned *The Story of Genji* in 1007. Mary Shelley, the wife of a renowned poet, was more than a little off the rose-strewn Victorian way when she wrote *Frankenstein*. Fantasy had been around since *Beowulf,* perhaps, but it took Hugo Gernsback to set the publishing world on its soon-to-be pointed ear with science fiction. All these artists, and many successful creators like them, possess something beyond talent—they have passion.

Every single day people around the world create or discover beautiful, remarkable, and sometimes totally bizarre works of art, music, literature, or science. I tend to buy a ticket to the show and stand back to marvel. But that's just me. What about you? Do you feel passionate about creating—in any genre? Dare to step off the beaten path if that's where inspiration beckons. Pick up a lightning rod, why don't you? Who's to say the next lightning bolt of inspiration isn't headed your way?

It worked for Benjamin Franklin.

Angels Bending Near Earlene

I've seen Capra's It's a Wonderful Life at least a dozen times, but I'd never experienced a holiday miracle of my own until one dark December night a few years ago. On that almost-Christmas eve, I encountered an angel—a couple of them, in fact—and learned a lesson in faith, prayer, and God's love that I will never forget. This is a true story. Only the names have been changed—and not all of them!

"It's Christmas," I reminded myself under my breath. "Peace on earth. Goodwill to men." Supposing the heavenly exhortation extended to children as well, I looped the piece of cloth around a little shepherd's head instead of tying it around his mouth as I'd have liked to.

It was already December twenty-somethingth, and I had yet to bake a tray of cookies or wrap a single gift.

Instead, I'd spent most of the month writing a Christmas pageant, assigning parts, sewing and refurbishing costumes, building a stable, affixing a star in the cultural hall firmament, and directing twenty-some kids who were all now sugar-filled and giddy at the thought of Santa's imminent arrival.

Despite being on the verge of a nervous breakdown, I was pleased. It was our night of nights at last, and we were ready. By the time the bishop stood to welcome the audience and announce the opening prayer, the set was decorated, the choir assembled, and the characters in place. Everyone and everything looked wonderful.

Having just completed my last task—shoving a crown on a wise guy's little head for the umpteenth time—I slumped against the wall in the back of the cultural hall to enjoy the fruits of my labors. Just then a door flew open and an excited, windblown little girl ran into the room and grabbed my hand with her icy fingers. It was Earlene. As if the name alone wasn't enough for a ten-year-old to contend with, this little girl was painfully thin, wore thick glasses, and had incredibly prominent teeth. She also had one of the strongest, sweetest personalities I'd ever encountered. I wondered if that was the reason she'd been sent to the family she had—one that seemed to have more than its share of trials in life.

"How do I look?" she asked breathlessly. "Where do I go for my part?"

She looked like she'd just tumbled off a hayride, but I didn't tell her that. Nor did I mention that she might have known what was going on if she'd made it to even one practice.

After assuring Earlene she looked beautiful, I nudged her toward a children's choir that was assembled around the piano. At least I tried to nudge her. She wouldn't move.

"No!" she cried, pushing her heavy glasses back up the bridge of her nose. "I'm an angel!"

People in the last few rows forgot that Brother Crawford was now pronouncing a blessing upon the proceedings and turned to look at us instead.

"You're not an angel," I whispered. I had no idea where she'd gotten the idea in the first place. Then I added encouragingly, "But you're a very important part of the choir." Never mind that she wouldn't know any of the songs since she attended Primary too seldom to learn them.

I'd dragged her about six inches closer to the choir before she yanked her hand from mine. "You said!" she insisted. "You said in church that I'm supposed to be an angel!"

My mouth opened, but no words came out of it. I was trying to remember just what I'd said to her and when. I seemed to recall speaking to Earlene in the hallway a couple of weeks previously. I'd been in a rush to get to Sunday School before my students and had practically knocked her into a wall. Whatever I had said then had been an apology . . . and perhaps a platitude.

"You said I'm an angel!" Earlene wailed.

The audience uttered a resounding, "Amen!" I hoped it was in response to the end of the prayer.

I looked down into two myopic little eyes and knew it was possible—probable, even—that I had called Earlene an angel. But I certainly hadn't meant she was a Christmas-pageant angel. I'd meant she was a . . . well, you know.

Earlene didn't know. She only knew that since I was director of the pageant, God had given me the right to appoint little girls to be His heavenly messengers for ten or fifteen minutes in that particular ward on that particular night. Clearly, being chosen as an angel for the Christmas pageant—or believing that she had been—was the best thing that had ever happened in her short and surely difficult life.

Earlene clasped my hand again with both of hers, and her eyes shone. "I've asked Heavenly Father every night to help me be a perfect angel in His pageant. He *will* help me. I know He will."

The thought of Earlene's sweet, fervent prayers brought tears to my eyes, but there was nothing I could do. The pageant would begin any second. I prayed for words to explain to the little girl that she had misunderstood, but there were no words in any language that could fix this. No matter what I said, Earlene would still believe in her heart that God had handpicked her to be an angel.

She looked from me to the softly lit stage and back again, clearly wondering when I'd produce that white robe and silver garland worn by the other pageant angels.

At any moment, the welling in my eyes was going to run down my cheeks. There was no doubt in my mind that this misunderstanding would drive her parents even further from the Church. Worse, might the awful disappointment cause Earlene to wonder if God heard her prayers? Would she now wonder why, if God *did* hear her, He would ignore her hopes and happiness . . . and at Christmas?

Despite my fears of a family's impending apostasy and a child's crisis of faith, I simply didn't have an angel costume—or any way to come up with one in two minutes or less. My thoughts raced. Earlene wore a dirty orange sweatshirt and tattered blue jeans. No way could I slip her onstage with the robe-clad girls without evoking stares and giggles that would break her heart. I looked frantically around the room, hoping to spot a shirt or a sweater or anything white that

I could strip off an unsuspecting ward member. While everybody looked festive, nobody looked angelic.

The Relief Society room was locked, or I would have ripped the tablecloth out from under the pot of poinsettias and improvised. At that point I might have considered packing Earlene in snow, but we were in Arizona, so I didn't have any of that either.

Heedless of Longfellow's bells tolling despair back in the corner, the pianist broke into "Joy to the World," and the first narrator entered. The play had begun.

An awful understanding began to creep onto Earlene's face. The census was going forth from Caesar Augustus, and she was going nowhere. "Hurry!" she said. "I need my costume now! I have to go be with the angels!"

I wanted to "go be with the angels" too, but my wish was metaphorical. I simply wanted to die before I had to witness the shattering of Earlene's heart.

Just then, Sister Morgan appeared in a doorway not six feet from where Earlene and I stood. If she had been the angel Moroni materializing with a golden trump in hand, I couldn't have been more surprised. In her hand was a hanger, and on the hanger was a clean, white angel costume that was exactly Earlene's size.

Earlene had her shoes off, her jeans rolled to the knees, and the robe on before I managed to draw a single breath. With a dazzling smile on her face, she raced across the room and hoisted herself onto the stage. Although clearly surprised at her sudden arrival, one of the "regular" angels ripped half the garland from her own belt and used it to adorn Earlene's long, hopelessly-tangled hair.

Angels are like that. Bless their little hearts.

When the program ended, I was still standing in the same spot, and I was crying in earnest. It was the best Christmas pageant ever. Mary and Joseph had made it all the way to Bethlehem without bickering as they had done in every rehearsal. The shepherds had neither dueled with their staffs nor played keep-away with their stuffed sheep. The wise men had found their way from the East without a detour to the drinking fountain. And above them all stood the angels—beautiful, bright, beatific—with Earlene in the very front. I will always believe there was a surreal glow—and maybe an extra angel or two—around her.

When I could speak again, I sought out Sister Morgan. Sue had no idea she'd just pulled off the biggest Christmas miracle since Clarence earned his wings. When I asked her where she'd come up with the costume, she reminded me that I'd given it to her daughter the year before. Only then did I remember being impressed to let the little girl keep the robe when she asked, but I certainly had never expected to see it again.

Several times during the year, Sue told me, she'd almost thrown away the angel costume, but something made her stuff it back in the closet instead of dropping it into the wastebasket. The same something had urged her to find it after dress rehearsal and wash and press it. In the end, she'd left it behind in her haste to get her children to the church on time, but that stubborn, blessed "something" had intervened one last time. Sue had gotten up out of her seat, hurried home to grab the costume, and then returned just as the pageant began.

I was awestruck by the heavenly machinations. I had been prompted to give away a costume I wanted to keep. Sue had been impressed to keep a costume she didn't want. These minor miracles, set in place hundreds of days before, wouldn't impact the world. They were all for the benefit of one little girl—a child who loved her Heavenly Father and put her trust in Him. Because of her prayers, Earlene was a perfect angel that night. Or at least she was a pageant angel . . . with perfect faith.

The real miracle, of course, is the one of which prophets and apostles testify: the infinite love God has for each of His children. Elder Jeffrey R. Holland said, "I do not know exactly how He does it, but I testify to you that He knows us and loves us individually and that He hears our prayers. My testimony is that nothing in this universe is more important to Him than your hopes and happiness."[30]

I gained this testimony firsthand one beautiful, blessed near-Christmas night. Our Father—who loved us all enough to send His Son—loved odd little Earlene enough to send her an angel robe. He had known her prayers months and months before she uttered them and had set in motion a plan to reward her innocent faith before she exercised it.

And so it is with us. Each year when children sing, "Be near me, Lord Jesus, I ask thee to stay close by me forever, and love me, I pray," I feel the warm, prickling confirmation of the Spirit and think of Earlene. I don't know where she is now, but I suspect that she is still a perfect angel, still close to her Heavenly Father, and still looked over and loved by He who blesses each of us so perfectly.

I like to think that Earlene still has her white robe. I gave it to her, of course. It's all she asked Santa for that night when she sat upon his lap. Besides, "something" told me that angel costume had been made and preserved and protected just for her.

Just *like* her.

---

[30] Holland, Jeffrey R., "Considering Covenants: Women, Men, Perspective, Promises," in Susette Fletcher Green and Dawn Hall Anderson, eds., *To Rejoice as Women: Talks from the 1994 Women's Conference* (Salt Lake City: Deseret Book Company, 1995), 96–97.

Pennies in the Water

When a good friend of mine returned from a mission, she wrote:

While I was in New York we went to a Chinese place and I got a fortune that said, "Travel this year will give you a new perspective on life." I laughed, but kept the fortune. I really hate that we can't see the end result of the things we do now. I want to know what perspective I've gained. Mom says I'm different, but I feel the same. So what changed? What was the purpose of me going on a mission? Was it for me to change the world or for the world—and God—to change me?

Like Kristy, the talented, inspired young woman who wrote those words, I wonder about my life-mission. Specifically, with every book I publish, I wonder about writing. Have I been granted this wondrous opportunity because of what I have to give or because it will open windows to what I need to receive?

I tend to think it's that second thing. I receive so much. Near the top of the list of things I get is letters. I get a lot of letters, more than half of them from young women. I always answer, sometimes more than once. Sometimes I answer more than a dozen times. I've been answering some for so long now that I've received wedding invitations and birth announcements from women who were Beehives or Mia Maids when they read my first book. It is one of the greatest marvels—and joys—in my life. If these friendships were all I ever got from writing, I would consider myself not only duly rewarded for the hours at the keyboard, but also richly blessed.

But I get more. Just last week, for instance, I got a moving lesson in humility. One of the many online sites that encourage book reviews had a post from someone who said she was "sorry" to say it, but she thought one of my novels was the worst book published on this—or any other—planet. (She didn't *sound* sorry, by the way. She sounded absolutely delighted to point out my literary shortcomings.)

Despite the fact that there were six stellar reviews alongside the one negative, guess which one I've memorized? (Why am I like that? And while we're on the subject, somebody please tell me I'm not the only one who is!) Anyway, it affected me so negatively I could scarcely look at a newly edited book that had just come back for review. Even the thought of publishing another novel made me cringe. I mean, what if the new one was as "bad" as the old one? What if it was *worse*? Why jeopardize a rainforest—or in the case of my print runs, a couple of scraggly pine trees—when the world has enough inanity (and to spare) already?

As it turns out, I found the answer to that question in the latter part of Kristy's letter. She related a story about being on Temple Square with a little boy who was visiting Salt Lake City. They were looking together into one of the many reflecting pools where tourists toss coins. When the child observed that the money wasn't doing anybody any good in there and that he could better use it, Kristy explained the old custom of tossing pennies into the water in order to make a wish. Then she added that nobody—especially good little Primary kids—should reach in to take the money.

The little boy nodded solemnly and said, "Because you don't want to steal anybody's hopes!"

Kristen concluded, "It was so funny! As if taking coins from a pool could affect people's dreams. But what if it does? That would be a good lesson—not to steal from wishing wells."

I think my words are like those coins. Perhaps many of them really aren't doing anybody any good—and yet I've tossed them out into the world's reflecting pool with the best of intentions. They're my way of wishing well to anyone who happens upon them. With every book I write, I wish that good could always triumph over evil. I wish that everyone could live happily ever after. At the very least, I wish that we would all laugh more than we cry and get up one more time than we fall down.

I know it's a lot to wish for. Nevertheless, I have a whole handful of coins left to me, and I'm going to keep tossing them into that pool just as long as I can lift my arm.

There is a quote by Washington Irving taped to my computer:

Methinks I hear the questions asked by my graver readers, "To what purpose is all this—how is the world to be made wiser by this talk?" Alas! Is there not wisdom enough extant for the instruction of the world? And if not, are there not thousands of abler pens labouring for its improvement? It is so much pleasanter to please than to instruct—to play the companion rather than the preceptor.

What, after all, is the mite of wisdom that I could throw into the mass of knowledge; or how am I sure that my sagest deductions may be safe guides for the opinions of others? But in writing to amuse, if I fail, the only evil is in my own disappointment. If, however, I can by any lucky chance, in these days of evil, rub out one wrinkle from the brow of care, or beguile the heavy heart of one moment of sorrow; if I can now and then penetrate through the gathering film of misanthropy, prompt a benevolent view of human nature, and make my reader more in good humour with his fellow-beings and himself, surely, surely, I shall not then have written entirely in vain.[31]

Perhaps I never will, as Irving said, "contribute a mite to the wisdom and knowledge of the world." I can live with that. In fact, I can rejoice as long as I am able to let go of the pressure to impress and replace it with a desire to serve, coupled with a deep appreciation for the myriad of blessings I receive every day—just for trying.

As now we part, Gentle Reader, I leave you with the scripture I have written somewhere where I know I'll never misplace it—upon the tablets of my heart. It's

---

[31] Irving, Washington, "Christmas Dinner," in *Old Christmas* (New York: Putnam & Sons, 1888).

only eight words long, but they are words that have shaped my life as no others:

Be still, and know that I am God.
(Psalm 46:10)

This world we share is a place of infinite beauty and wonder. The paths we choose can lead to eternal life. Truly, "eye hath not seen, nor ear heard, neither have entered into the heart of man, the things which God hath prepared for them that love him" (1 Corinthians 2:9). We need only be still long enough to remember who we are . . . and *whose* we are. Every day—in joy and sorrow and triumph and devastation and all that seemingly endless busy-ness that is part and parcel of a woman's sphere—we must calm ourselves long enough to gaze deeply into the reflecting pool of the Spirit. When we do, we will *always* see the tender mercies of our God, sparkling before us like newly minted pennies in the water.

About the Author

An Arizona native, Kerry Blair lives with her husband and mother in Chino Valley, where she passes time counting stars, chickens (after they've hatched), and her many blessings. To break the monotony of such an idyllic rural life, she often speaks at firesides, conferences, and enrichment meetings across the Southwest. (For a schedule and/or to invite her to speak, please visit her website, kerryblair.com.)

Kerry has published eight novels with Covenant, but *Counting Blessings* is her first full-length work of non-fiction. Since one of her avocations is corresponding with readers, she can be reached through her website, kerryblair.com; by email, kerrylynnblair@aol.com; through Covenant email, info@covenant-lds.com; or through snail mail, care of Covenant Communication, Inc., Box 416, American Fork, UT 84003-0416. Things are slow in Chino Valley, so she *always* responds.